Emerging Dimensions in Self-Help Groups

Emerging Dimensions in Self-Help Groups

N. Mukundan
M. Hilaria Soundari

Dominant Publishers and Distributors
NEW DELHI-110002

Emerging Dimensions in Self-Help Groups

ISBN 81-7888-518-2

Dominant Publishers and Distributors

Editorial Office :

116–A, South Anarkali, Delhi - 110051.

Ph. 22415687.

Sales & Marketing :

4378/4-B, Murari Lal Street, Ansari Road,

Daryaganj, New Delhi - 110002.

Ph. 23281685, Fax. 91-11-23270680.

Production:

199/5, C.B. Marg, Moujpur, Delhi - 110053.

Ph. 22913460.

e-mail: dominantbooks@post.com

Published by. A.S. Saini for Dominant Publishers And Distributors.
Printed at Orient Offset, Delhi - 110053.

Foreword

From time immemorial, saving habit has been embedded in our societal value system. The dynamics of modern Self-Help Groups (SHGs), based on the Bangladeshi Grammen Bank model with microcredit delivery mechanism, has actually revolutionized the livelihoods of the less privileged sections in society. A SHG is a distinct self-governed, peer controlled informal group of powerless people with similar socio-economic setting and having a propensity to collectively perform a Common Mini(maxi)mum Programme (CMP) *i.e.*, to empower themselves economically so as to empower others socially.

In the Indian context, NABARD launched the SHG-Bank Linkage programme on a pilot basis in February, 1992. Since then, the linkage between Banks and SHGs with the NGOs as facilitators/financial intermediaries, as a mechanism for channeling microcredit to the poor on a sustainable basis offer a package of potential economic as well as social advantages. Women's empowerment, entrepreneurship and poverty reduction are the hallmarks of the operational dynamics of SHGs throughout the country.

The compendium of "Emerging Dimensions in Self-Help Groups" contains the overall dimensions as well as specific functional aspects of SHGs with sectoral empirical orientations. The contents and coverage from various campus academics have shown how the impactional role of SHGs made perceptible changes in the living standards of the socially marginalized groups in our traditional society.

I appreciate the young academics, Mr. N. Mukundan of A.V.C. College (Autonomous) Mayiladuthurai and Dr. M. Hilaria Soundari of Gandhigram Rural Institute (Deemed University), Gandhigram for their sincere efforts in bringing out a volume on a socially relevant topical interest. The book is a very useful referral to students, researchers, social activists, rural development catalysts and policy pundits on the dimensions and dynamics of SHGs.

A genuine teacher should go beyond a class room and enlarge the scope of his/her academic activities. Wish the authors to bring more books which are beneficial to the academic community.

Dr. P. Jegadish Gandhi
Founder—Director
Vellore Institute of Development Studies (VIDS), Vellore.
Academic Council Member: Vellore Institute of Technology (VIT) and Thiruvalluvar University, Vellore

Preface

At present time it widely recognized that the concept of Self Help Groups is made silent revolution in rural India. Over the past five decades 'trickle down' strategy was left out vast majority of rural folk. In other words, the fruits of development strategy failed to reach the marginalized people. The majority of the neglected poor are landless agricultural workers, small farmers etc. Further the burden of poverty falls heavily on women, who shoulder the work load in poor household with less access to education, health and remunerative active. In this scenario, the great challenge is to develop a village centered development strategy for the marginalized and rural poor. U.N. Millennium Development Goals also stress on empowerment of women and reduction of poverty.

The present volume focuses its attention on the matters that demand urgent action themes such as the emerging dimensions strategies and future vision of SHGs. Moreover empowerment of women tribal development sustainable rural development and women entrepreneurship through SHGs also are vividly enumerated.

The collection of articles is a great task but the generous mind and assistance given by the numerous eminent scholars from all over India made it easy to do so. We are extremely happy for the opportunity to engage in this intellectual venture.

We thank all the authors who have graciously responded to our humble request and contributed articles, which can expand the horizon of knowledge. We acknowledge that the response went beyond our expectations. We do express our gratitude to them for their kind help rendered to us in achieving a noble endeavour.

We express our deep sense of gratitude to renowned economist Dr. P. Jegadish Gandhi, Director, Vellore Institute of Development Studies, Vellore, T.N. for writing a foreword to this book. We are extremely grateful to Dr. G. Chandrakumar, Reader and Head, Dept. of Economics, A.V.C. College (Autonomous), Mayiladuthurai, T.N., Dr. M.A. Sudhir, Prof. & Head, Dept. of Applied Research, Gandhigram Rural Institute, Deemed University, Dindigul, T.N. for his constant blessing, inspiration and valuable suggestions in bringing out this book.

We particularly like to place on record our deep sense of gratitude to Mr. K. Senthilnayagam, Librarian, A.V.C. College (Autonomous), Mayiladuthurai, T.N. who is a source of inspiration and for making efforts to contact the publishers.

We appreciate the co-operation and support of Mr. A. S. Saini, Director, Dominant Publication for publishing this book with due patience, care and interest.

Above all, we would like to thank God for his grace and guidance from the inception till the completion of this intellectual work.

—N. Mukundan
—Dr. M. Hilaria Soundari

List of Contributors

1. **Mr. N. Mukundan**

   Lecturer in Economics
   P.G. and Research Department of Economics
   A.V.C. College (Autonomous)
   Mannanpandal,
   Mayiladuthurai, Tamil Nadu.

2. **Dr. M. Hilaria Soundari**

   Lecturer in Applied Research
   Department of Applied Research
   Gandhigram Rural Institute (Deemed University)
   Gandhigram, Dindigul District, Tamil Nadu.

3. **Dr. G. Chandrakumar**

   Reader and Head
   P.G. and Research Department of Economics
   A.V.C. College (Autonomous),
   Mannanpandal,
   Mayiladuthurai, Tamil Nadu.

4. **Dr. A. Ramalingam**

   Reader in Economics
   P.G. and Research Department of Economics
   A.V.C. College (Autonomous),
   Mannanpandal,
   Mayiladuthurai, Tamil Nadu.

5. **Dr. Gautam Purkayastha**

   Prof. & Head
   Department of Economics
   Margherita College
   Margherita, Assam.

6. **Prof. V. Sekar**

   Prof. and Head
   Department of Social Sciences
   Horticultural College Research Institute
   Periyakulam,
   Tamil Nadu.

7. **Dr. Santha Govind**

   Prof. of Agricultural Extension
   Department of Agriculture
   Faculty of Agriculture
   Annamalai University
   Annamalai Nagar,
   Tamil Nadu.

8. **Mr. D. Vengatesan**

   Lecturer in Agriculture Extension
   Department of Agriculture
   Faculty of Agriculture
   Annamalai University
   Annamalai Nagar,
   Tamil Nadu.

9. **Dr. R. Haridoss**

   Prof. and Head
   Department of Mathematical Economics
   School of Economics
   Madurai Kamaraj University
   Madurai, Tamil Nadu.

10. **Dr. B. Vijayachandran Pillai**

Reader in Commerce
P.G. and Research Department of Commerce
VTM NSS College
Dhanuvachapuram,
Thiruvanathapuram, Kerala.

11. **Dr. V. Harikumar**

Reader in Commerce
P.G. and Research Department of Commerce
Mahatma Gandhi College
Thiruvanathapuram, Kerala.

12. **Dr. M. Anbalagan**

Reader and Head
P.G. and Research Department of Commerce
Voorhees College
Vellore, Tamil Nadu.

13. **Mr. V. Selvam**

Sr. Lecturer in Management
V.I.T. Business School
Vellore Institute of Technology
Vellore, Tamil Nadu.

14. **Mrs. K. Kalaichelvi**

Lecturer in Commerce
P.G. and Research Department of Commerce
St. Joseph College (Autonomous)
Trichy, Tamil Nadu.

15. **Mr. J. Fredrick**

Lecturer in Economics
Department of Economics
N.M.S.S. Vellaichamy Nadar College
Madurai.

16. **Dr. R. Karthikeyan**

Lecturer in Economics
P.G. and Research Department of Economics
A.V.C. College (Autonomous),
Mannanpandal,
Mayiladuthurai, Tamil Nadu.

17. **Dr. K. Ramakrishnan**

Lecturer in Commerce
P.G. and Research Department of Commerce
A.V.C. College (Autonomous),
Mannanpandal,
Mayiladuthurai, Tamil Nadu.

18. **G. Narayanan**

Ph.D. Scholar
IARI, New Delhi.

19. **V. Saravanakumar**

Teaching Assistant
Dept. of Social Sciences
Horticultural College Research Institute
Periyakulam, Tamil Nadu.

20. **R. Selvam**

Ph.D. Scholar
P.G. and Research Department of Economics
A.V.C. College (Autonomous),
Mannanpandal,
Mayiladuthurai, Tamil Nadu.

21. **S. Dharmaraj**

Ph.D. Scholar
P.G. and Research Department of Economics
A.V.C. College (Autonomous),
Mannanpandal,
Mayiladuthurai, Tamil Nadu.

22. **C. Suguna**

Ph.D. Scholar
P.G. and Research Department of Economics
A.V.C. College (Autonomous),
Mannanpandal,
Mayiladuthurai, Tamil Nadu.

23. **Miss B. Sumathi**

M.Phil. Research Scholar
P.G. and Research Department of Economics
A.V.C. College (Autonomous)
Mannanpandal,
Mayiladuthurai, Tamil Nadu.

Contents

Part—II

Women Empowerment : Proactive Role of SHGs

Contents

Part—II

Women Empowerment : Proactive Role of SHGs

Part—III

SHGs : Sectoral Studies

Part—I

Dynamics of Self-Help Groups (SHGs) : An Overview

Chapter—1

Emerging Dimensions in Self-Help Groups— An Introduction

*—Mr. N. Mukundan**

Over the years a plethora of poverty alleviation programmes are not reaching the ultimate beneficiaries. In other words, an approach of top level planning did not consider the needs and requirements of the needy. As a result, still 25 percent of population is poverty-stricken which is no doubt that the resources used for poverty alleviation and of subsidies in the name of poor have not been much effective in achieving the goal of elimination of poverty. Further, the rural development programmes relating to agriculture and allied activities had short lived. Consequently the result of vicious circle of poverty, are low production, low employment, seasonal migration and increased suicidal rates. But leaders, academics and civil servants are baffled by the

* Lecturer in Economics, Post Graduate and Research Department of Economics, A.V.C. College (Autonomous) Mannampandal, Mayiladuthurai, Tamil Nadu.

continuous failure of rural programmes. In this context, the concept of SHGs has emerged as a panacea for current rural problems.

SHGs are the outcome of the Grameen Bank of Bangladesh, which was founded by Prof. Mohammed Yenans in 1975. It is group of homogenous members of the needy people who meet the consumption of day today life of its members from its own savings and collective fund generated among themselves. The main activities of the SHGs are participation, planning, resource mobilization, self-management and mutual help.

The major target populations under this category of marginalized people are like landless agriculture laborers, marginal peasants, rural crafts person and small traders. The representative of the group successfully conduct meetings and frame interventional strategies.

Improving the skills and abilities of people to enable them to manage better, with existing development delivery systems. The empowerment process encompasses several mutually reinforcing components like economic independence, awareness, self-image and autonomy. Providing micro credit to the rural women through an organized set up have made them entrepreneur. Thus, SHGs have enhanced the equal status of women as participants, decision makers and beneficiaries in development activities. It is a tool for encouraging the rural women to take active participation in development activities. Gandhiji said, "Train a man and you train an individual; train a woman and you build a nation." It is really opt Self-Help Groups.

SHGs empower women and train them to take active part in the training programmes like gender sensitization, personality development and leadership. They are relieved of their superstitions and other social limitations. At present, SHGs have made a great confidence in the minds of rural women to succeed in their day-to-day life. It is certainly can contribute for socio-economic development of rural India.

Economic emancipation of rural women are made effective with the process self employment programmes. As self-employment is the only best alternative available to make the rural women empowered through SHGs and it can stimulate the process of sustainable rural development.

Chapter—2

SHGs in Kerala—An Evaluation

*—Dr. B. Vijayachandran Pillai**

*—Dr. V. Harikumar***

INTRODUCTION

Indian Economy is an Agrarian One. More then 70 percent of the people depend on agriculture and allied activities for their livelihood. Agricultural activities are deeply concentrated in rural areas. However, unemployment, underemployment and subsequent poverty are common in the rural areas of the country. The Government of India has formulated different innovative schemes and strategies to mitigate the problems that prevail in the rural sector.

* Reader in Commerce, Post Graduate and Research Department of Commerce, VTMNSS College, Dhanuvachapuram, Thiruvanathapuram, Kerala,

** Reader in Commerce, Post Graduate and Resarch Department of Commerce, Mahatma Gandhi College, Thiruvanathapuram, Kerala.

The Community Development Projects, the National Extension Service Scheme of 1950s, the Intensive Agricultural District programme and the Intensive Area Development Programme of 1960s were a few directed towards the uplift of the poor and the marginalized sections of the Society. In addition to these, programmes like TRYSEM, NREP, RLEGP etc. were designed and targeted exclusively for the upliftment of rural poor and weaker sections. In spite of these efforts, poverty still remains in our country and is becoming severe and acute, posing problems to our economy as a whole.

The State of Kerala is one of the backward States of India. Though the State has initiated many developmental endeavours, unemployment and poverty still persist in the State. Certain remarkable moves of the Government of Kerala such as land reforms, Public Distribution System with reasonable food security, introduction of Social Security Schemes etc. and remittance from emigrants have helped the State to eradicate the level of poverty and unemployment to some extent. However, the problems of poverty and unemployment have no abatement. Hence, the successive Governments framed and implemented many poverty alleviation programmes to address Poverty. Among the various programmes 'Swarnjayanti Gram Swarozgar Yojana' is a novel and dominant one. This programme was introduced in Kerala on 01.04.1999, at 75:25 cost sharing between the Central and State Governments. The basic objective of this programme is to improve the economic status and to bring the beneficiaries above the poverty line by providing income generating assets to them through bank credit and Government subsidy. Kerala is seeking to achieve a break through in the mission of poverty alleviation by earmarking a sizeable amount of fund in the budget allocation for the smooth implementation of this programme.

THE CONCEPT OF SELF HELP GROUP

Self Help Group (SHG) is a homogeneous group of poor people, women, users etc. This groups is a voluntary one formed on areas of common interest so that they can think, organized and operate for their development. SHGs function on the basis of co-operative principles and provide a forum for members to extent support to each other. It is considered as a means of empowerment. SHGs organize very poor people who do not have access to financial system in the organized sector. In groups, normally transparency and accountability are lacking. However, in a group like SHG, they are ensured through collective action of the members. This scheme mobilizes the poor rural people especially women to form groups for mutual benefits, SHGs play a crucial role in improving the savings and credit and also in reducing poverty and social inequalities.

SHGs can be formed with 5 to 10 members. The Groups can avail themselves of financial facilities offered by the financial institutions and the Government. The individual members can also apply for the credit facilities. However, there are certain norms and prescribed procedures for obtaining credit. Frequently, the group should convene meetings of its members and discuss all the issues relating to the groups on a common platform. This provides an opportunity to members to express freely their views, expectations and suggestions for improving the functioning of the group. Regularly, Government agencies and Voluntary Development Organisations organize training programmes enable the members to learn, co-operate and work in a group environment. SHGs are required to maintain records as directed by the monitoring agencies.

OBJECTIVES AND METHODOLOGY

The main objective of the present paper is to identify the main problems faced by the SHGs operating in the State of Kerala and to suggest a few feasible solutions to tackle problems. For achieving this objective, the methodology adopted is stated below.

The Study is mainly based on the Primary Data. However, for gaining a good background, Secondary Data were also used. The Primary data required for the preparation of this paper are collected from the selected SHGs functioning throughout the State of Kerala. A survey was conducted among these SHGs and the Data were collected by discussing with the members of the Groups. Moreover, interviews and discussion were held with the officials of the Rural Development Department, Government of Kerala to elicit the valuable data for the purpose of the Study.

MAJOR FINDINGS OF THE SURVEY

As per survey data, the following are the major problem of SHGs in Kerala.

Raw Material Problems

SHGs use locally available raw materials for producing finished products. Normally, they fulfill these requirements by approaching local suppliers. As they purchase raw materials in smaller quantities from the local suppliers, they are denied of getting the benefits of discount, credit facility etc. Due to financial shortage, they are not able to find genuine and competent raw material suppliers operating in nearby areas to get raw materials supply regularly. Sometimes they are forced to buy substandard raw material at higher prices. These drawbacks force them to produce products of low quality and charge a higher price for the finished products.

Financial Problems

Financial problem is very common and acute among SHGs in Kerala. It arises due to two different reasons. The prominent among them is the inadequate financial support from the external agencies like Banks operating in different sectors. Moreover, the financial aid given by them to these groups is very meager. The financial support extended by these agencies is not adequate to meet the actual requirements of these groups. The second reason for the financial problem of SHGs is due to the weak financial management of the members of the groups. It is found that in certain units, the return from the business is not properly reinvested in the units for its sustained growth. Diversion of funds for personal and domestic purposes like marriage, construction of houses are not uncommon among the groups functioning in the State.

Marketing Problems

Marketing is a sensitive functional area. Business can survive and flourish only if they can market the finished products successfully. SHGs in Kerala are not able to discharge the marketing functions commendably on account of the reasons such as insufficient orders, lack of linkage with marketing agencies, lack of adequate sales promotion measures, lack of permanent market for the products of SHGs. Absence of proper brand name, poor and unattractive packing system, poor quality of products due to the application of traditional technology, stiff competition from other major participants, lack of well defined and well knit channel of distribution of marketing etc. Unless and otherwise the members of this group consider and address these aspects seriously, it would become a cause for their decline.

Production Problems

For producing products, the members of the group usually depend on outdated and second hand technology. This will hamper the smooth functioning of the units. Certain units are using new machinery available in the market. However, the members of the groups are not able to use these production techniques successfully. Inadequate training facilities is cited as one the reasons for this handicap. These inadequate training facilities also create some problems for the members in certain aspects like product selection, maintenance of quality of products, performing managerial functions etc. As a result, SHGs are not able to compete with small units functioning within the State and neighbouring States.

Problems Related with Members

Illiteracy is a major problem of rural masses. As a result of this, the members of the group are not familiar with the schemes beneficial to them formulated by the Government. Now Government of Kerala offers subsidies and other schemes of assistance up to a maximum of Rs. 5 Lakhs. However, many members of the group are ignorant about this provision. Moreover, it is found that in the case of a few units strong members' try to earn a lion's share of the profit of the group by exploiting the ignorant and illiterate members. In the case of SHGs dominated by women, it is found that there is no stability of the units as many married women are not in a position to associate with the group due to the shift of their place of residence. Moreover, there is no unity among women members owing to personal reasons.

Lack of Co-operation of Government Officials

The attitude of the officials of the Department of Rural Development is not encouraging. They are not well trained to accept the challenges and equip the SHGs self sufficient. Similarly, for getting assistance and support, the group members usually approach the line officers. However, the line officers are

not Co-operative with the SHGs. This will hamper the very objective of the schemes.

Insufficient Return

For the survival of the units a reasonable return on Investment is a pre-requisite. However, the Return on Investment (ROI) of SHGs is poor on account of various reasons like inefficient management, high cost of production, absence of quality consciousness, insufficient supply of financial aid, over dependence on money lenders etc.

SUGGESTIONS

The following suggestions are offered improving the present situation of SHGs in the State of Kerala.

1. As a solution to the problem of raw material, in a particular area separate SHGs can be formed for procuring and supplying of raw materials required for the other SHGs operating in that area. Moreover, in the State of Kerala there are plenty of locally available resources and the information about locally available raw material and their varied uses may be disseminated to SHGs. Proper encouragement and training should be provided to them to produce innovative products by using these materials. In order to have a knowledge base about the availability of materials, in Panchayat levels, surveys can be conducted under the auspices of local authorities.
2. For solving the problems of marketing of SHGs, the Kerala Rural Development and Marketing Society (KERAMS) should extend their activities throughout the State of Kerala instead of limiting its operation in a particular area. Further, various SHGs functioning in a particular Panchayat area can form a Co-operative Society. This so-

ciety may be entrusted with the task of marketing of various products of SHGs under a common brand name. The society can perform various sales promotion activities and procure rare raw materials for the benefit of the member SHGs.

3. Non-Governmental Organisations can play a vital role in empowering women entrepreneurs and other male members by providing basic education, motivation, training, financial aid an so on. All the members of the SHGs may not have the same caliber and expertise. Non-Government Organizations can identify the inefficient member of the group and can impart proper training to them in order to make them competent. For this purpose, short term training programmes can be arranged at the Panchayat level.
4. The authorities of the Department of Rural Development can organize awareness camps frequently with a view to create awareness about the different schemes of assistance available to the members of SHGs.
5. The Financial Institutions should provide adequate financial assistance to the SHGs strictly on the basis of their actual performance without any discrimination of caste, politics, etc.

CONCLUSION

The very existence of SHGs is highly relevant to make the people below poverty line hopeful and self reliant. SHGs can play a crucial role to increase their income, improve their standard to living and status in society. It acts as a catalyst for bringing this section of the society to the main stream. Ultimately, the nation reaps the benefits of socialism.

Chapter—3

Self-Help Groups : A Study

*—Dr. G. Chandrakumar**

*—C. Suguna***

INTRODUCTION

Women play a significant and crucial role in number of sectors, *viz.*, dairy, horticulture, food processing, garments, handicrafts, fisheries, departmental stores, restaurants, beauty parlor, journalism, tourism, tax sources, financial services, Xerox services, telecom services, etc., Rural women have emerged as successful managers of earth's natural resources and they are responsible for more than half of the world's production from community based

* Reader and Head, Post Graduate and Research Department of Economics, A.V.C. College (Autonomous), Mannanpandal, Mayiladuthurai, Tamil Nadu.

** Ph.D. Scholar, Post Graduate and Resarch Department of Economics, A.V.C. College (Autonomous), Mannanpandal, Mayiladuthurai, Tamil Nadu.

enterprises. Women produce half of the world's food supply and account for 60% of the working force. Most women remain deprived of employment opportunities as wage workers because of their family responsibilities, lack of adequate skills and social and cultural barriers. In this context, self-employment or setting up enterprises of their own may become an opportunity for women to earn an income and acquire financial security. A shift from family management to enterprise management may be easier than a shift from paid employment to self-employment.

Most of the Women's enterprises tend to be home based because their Micro enterprises can serve four primary responsibilities as home makers with major objectives as:

1. Poverty reduction
2. Employment generation
3. Enterprises development, and
4. Empowerment of women

EMPOWERMENT OF WOMEN

The empowerment of women goes beyond increasing the income of women. The mobility of women and their access to information is strengthened by their process of participation in micro enterprises. Micro enterprise services contribute to an increased diversification of household economic activities, increased reliance on productive activities, and improved economic security. The Government has recognized the need for increased involvement of women in the main stream of economic development. The development of micro enterprises for women is an appropriate way to attack poverty at the grass root level by generating income. Self-Help Groups can play an effective role in promotion of micro enterprises.

GENESIS OF SELF HELP GROUPS

The Department, Ministry of Human Resource Development, Government of India, had initiated a new programme called Indira Mahila Yojana (IMY) in August 1995. Indira Mahila Yojana integrated components of several spectoral programmes and facilitated their convergence to benefit women. Women in the rural or urban areas were helped to form groups namely the Indira Mahila Kendras (IMKs) at the Anganwadi level. At the grass root level, Women's Self Help Groups were under every Anganwadi, which were later federated into the Indira Mahila Block Society (IMBS) to be registered under the Societies Act.

Self Help Groups (SHGs) adopt participatory approach for the socio-economic empowerment of women with a common objective to come together and participate in the development activities. Each Self-Help Group comprises of 15–20 women.

SOCIO-ECONOMIC EMPOWERMENT THROUGH SELF HELP GROUPS

At present, Self-Help Groups is widely used as an instrument to empower women socially and economically. Once Socio-economic empowerment is achieved, it would have implication on the overall development of women. The economic contribution of woman has been found to be related to her role and status in the society. Economic independence facilitates in bringing about sexual equality and increased income of women translates more directly into family well-being. Therefore, enhancing income earning opportunities through the formation of Self-Help Groups is a viable path way for empowerment of women.

Advantages through Self-Help Groups in The Villages and in The Community

- Inculcation of the spirit of Self Help
- Collective action for development
- Women begin to form similar groups seeing the success of the other Self-Help Groups
- Family welfare through social awareness of women
- Enhanced social status from secondary to primary
- Economic independence
- Voicing and acting against social injustices
- Problem solving ability
- Increased consciousness
- Desire for better infrastructure.

The data collected for the purpose of this study is secondary in nature. The study covers a period of six years from 1996–97 to 2001–2002. Compound growth rate is used to evaluate the progress of SHGs and bank linkage programme.

SHGs—BANK LINKAGE PROGRAMME IN TAMIL NADU AND INDIA

The micro credit programme was introduced in India in the year 1992. Over years since its inception, there has been a tremendous growth in respect of formation of SHGs, granting of bank loans and refinance through NABARD. Table 1 given below shows the progress of SHGs and bank linkage programme in India and Tamil Nadu.

It could be seen from the Table that the number of SHGs formed in India and Tamil Nadu for providing micro credit was increasing during the period from 1992 to 2002, the compound growth rate is being 119 percent and 124 percent respectively for India and Tamil Nadu. It is evident from the Table that the state had registered a better performance than that of the nation.

Similarly, banks were liberally granting loans through SHGs for meeting the micro credit needs. The amount of loan granted by the banks is on its increase during the last ten years.

Table 1. Progress of SHGs—Bank Linkage Programme in India and Tamil Nadu

	India		Tamil Nadu	
Year	No. of SHGs	Bank Loan (in Million)	No. of SHGs	Bank Loan (Rs. in Lakhs)
1992–1993	255	3	22	2,239
1993–1994	620	7	34	4,247
1994–1995	2,122	24	203	20,994
1995–1996	4,757	61	205	33,468
1996–1997	8,598	118	408	59,520
1997–1998	14,317	238	444	217,740
1998–1999	32,995	571	2,633	558,935
1999–2000	1,14775	1,930	7,715	1,958,237
2000–2001	2,63,825	4,809	16,926	5,37,523
2001–2002	4,61,478	10,263	27,539	10,463,598
Total	9,03,742	18,034	56,129	18,456,501
Compound Growth Rate	119%	146%	124%	154%

Source. NABARD.

With regard to the amount of loan granted to beneficiaries the growth rate for India and Tamil Nadu during the past ten years was 146 percent and 154 percent respectively. It is clear that the performance of Tamil Nadu is comparatively better than the performance at the national level in the implementation of micro credit programmes.

SHGs are formed as small functional groups in rural areas to increase the resource base of the members through the act of thrift and credit among themselves. They raise their corpus with credit support from services of banks and subsidy from government agencies concerned. To create quality groups, rural participation plays a pivotal role in identifying its members who are brought into the SHG-fold through the process of social mobilization. Functions of the groups are monitored and assessed by the external agencies with active support of Government, the lead bank of the region and Panchayat Union.

The SHGs formed and developed under various programmes provide a great opportunity for convergence of various programmes/activities of various Ministries and Organizations. The groups while aiming at promotion of savings and credit, should work as pressure groups to address social issues such as education, health, lack of access to natural resources, etc. Necessary training could be provided to the SHG members to create awareness on community health, traditional and modern agricultural practices, micro-credit, veterinary practices, water resource management, Panchayati Raj and other concerned. These trainings could be instrumental in increasing the abilities and confidence of the poor that may enable them for an effective contribution towards their own community development.

ECONOMIC EMPOWERMENT THROUGH INCOME GENERATING ACTIVITIES

Community based micro-enterprises like cotton coir rope making, coconut coir rope making, coconut leaf thatching, pickle manufacture, group leaf plate making, spices production, honey and food processing, agarbathi making etc. have proved to be most viable economic activities which would help to come out of the poverty trap in the rural areas. Here the products are consumed in the same locality. To sustain the community economic activities, leadership and membership training backed by participatory management is a must for the SHGs. The SHGs in this stage, if imparted entrepreneurial training combined with exposure visits to the successful micro-enterprise of the same nature would have a greater impact on the quality of the products produced by these poor beneficiaries.

There is no doubt that the success of the economic activities taken up by the self-employed persons largely depends on their social influence, their role in the decision making process, broader financial base through enhanced thrift and credit activities and widened ownership rights to the assets created by them. Thus, increased community solidarity has to be ensured to have a collective action and address location specific problems

EDUCATION

The members of the SHGs may be suitably involved in the on going Adult Education programme of the Department of Education where the Self-Employed members could be considered for training under Total Literacy Campaign (TLC)/Post Literacy Campaign (PLC)/ Continuing Adult Literacy Programme activities. In this endeavour, a major chunk of adult illiterate population could be systematically and comprehensively covered and would have a multiplier effect in increasing the performance of the literacy drive in the country. The following are the possible ways in which the objectives of literacy campaign in rural areas could be achieved through SHGs:

- The facilitators/ animators/Non-Government Organizations (NGOs) used in the formation and development of SHGs under SGSY may be sensitized of the benefits of Adult Education Programme in the sustainability of the group who may in turn disseminate necessary information amongst SHG members at the formation stage of the groups.
- Necessary training modules may be provided to resource persons who may visit the groups and disseminate requisite

information about the importance of education in taking up economic generation activities successfully under various schemes of the Government.

- The leader and the treasurer of the SHGs may be covered under the continuing education programme of Adult Education Programme in the first instance. This would motivate them to teach the remaining members.
- The District Rural Development Agencies (DRDAs) and district officials could be instructed to take necessary support from the line departments and Zila Saksharata Samitis (ZSS) in executing the objectives of National Literacy Mission (NLM) amongst the targeted SHGs. The existing infrastructure of the line department could also be utilized.
- Para-teachers, women literate volunteers (preferably amongst the SHGs) may be identified and recruited along with male volunteers who can visit remote and inaccessible areas and spread requisite awareness about adult education and can mobilize and motivate illiterate people to become economically sustainable by organizing into SHGs.
- Incentive to the groups may be awarded to who would successfully pass through the stages of adult Education Programme under NLM.

MID-DAY MEALS SCHEME

The National Programme of Nutritional Support to Primary Education, popularly known as Mid-Day Meals Scheme is under implementation in the country since August 1995 with an objective to ensure universalization of primary education by increasing enrolment and attendance and reducing school drop-out rates and simultaneously impacting on nutritional status of children in primary classes. There is an immense possibility of utilizing the services of the SHGs for

implementing the on-going mid-day meals scheme in different States. In this regard, quality and committed SHGs could be identified and a flexible decentralized approach be adopted for involving the members of these groups in cooking and supplying the mid-day meals to the school going children in the nearby primary schools. This endeavour would ensure successful implementation of the Centrally Sponsored Mid-day Meals Scheme by confirming timely and quality food supply to the children, while at the same time providing self employment opportunities to the Swarozgaris/members of Below Poverty Line (BPL) Self-Help Groups.

HEALTH

The services of SHGs could be tapped for eradication of major diseases like Tuberculosis (TB), Polio, Acquired Immuno Deficiency Syndrome (AIDS), which are common among the poor in rural areas. Similarly, the SHGs could play an instrumental role in the population stabilization programme of the Ministry of Health and Family Welfare through reaching the communication as well as benefits of these programmes to the BPL families, who tend to have large families, leading to higher dependency ratios. Maternal and Infant Mortality Rates are also high in these families. Mechanisms would need to be developed for Reproductive and Child Health (R.C.H) Programme benefits to reach the SHGs.

DEVELOPMENT OF CLUSTERS

Some organizations like Khadi & Village Industries Commission, Small Scale Industries, Ministry of Textiles, Development Commissioner, Handloom/Handicraft etc. have programmes for development of clusters in places where traditionally some activities have been going on. For example handloom, brass work. Carpet weaving, glass work, pottery, wood-craft, carving stone cane and bamboo, etc. are popular in some parts of the country. There is need to identify all such activities that could be taken up in clusters covering the groups of rural artisans in various areas. Cluster approach has the advantage of bringing in economies of scale as well as developing backward and forward linkages.

AGRICULTURE AND ALLIED ACTIVITIES

The agriculture extension programmes of the Ministry of Agriculture could be effectively implemented with the help of SHG members in the rural areas. Since 66% of the rural population is basically agrarian. Dairy, sheep breeding, poultry development are preferred activities among rural poor. The benefit of the activities can be maximized for the SHGs by ensuring appropriate forward and backward linkages with activities of the Department of Animal Husbandry & Dairy Development.

RURAL SANITATION

Various surveys on rural sanitation reveal that lack of appropriate awareness on health and hygiene in rural areas has lead to poor quality of life of the rural people. To improve the quality of life of the rural people and to ensure proper sanitation in rural areas, the Central Rural Sanitation Programme (CRSP) was launched in 1986 with an objective to ensure reduction in mortality and other diseases in rural India. The successful achievement of objectives of rural sanitation campaign depends largely on community mobilization and active participation of the members of the community in the sanitation related activities. Community organizations like SHGs could be asked to take up the activity of dissamination of necessary awareness on sanitation procedures in rural India.

CONCLUSION

True development is achieved only when the community's plans and actions take into account the roles and the potential opportunities for its present and future stakeholders. Sustainable Development rightly recognizes that all decisions pertaining to development must simultaneously consider various aspects of Economy, Environment, Equity and Society. It is the Community that can effectively guarantees the integrity of our human and natural resources. To conclude, we may say that the SHGs formed under various programmes provide a great scope for convergence of the programmes/activities of various Ministries/ Departments/Organizations which can look towards the SHGs for targeting their programmes, which ultimately would help in improving the quality of life in rural areas.

REFERENCES

- Nadarajan S., Ponmurugan R., "***Bank Linkage Programme***", ***Kisan World*** Vol. 33, No. 2, February 2006.
- Sagunthalai A., K. Ramakrishnan and S. Mahendran, "***Socio-Economic Emperiment of Women***" ***Kisan World*** Vol. 33, No. 7, July 2006.
- Tripathy K. K., "***A Catalyst of Rural Development***," ***Kurushetra***, Vol. 52, No. 8, June 2004.

Chapter—4

Working of SHGs—A Case from Tamil Nadu

—Dr. G. Chandrakumar*
—R. Selvam**

INTRODUCTION OF THE STUDY

Swarnjayanti Gram Swarozgar Yojana (SGSY), will focus on organization of the poor at grassroots level through a process of social mobilization for poverty eradication. SGSY's approach to organization of the poor stems from the conviction that there is a tremendous potential within the poor to help themselves and that the potential can be harnessed by organizing them. Social mobilization enables the poor to build their own organizations (self-help groups) in which they

* Reader and Head, Post Graduate and Research Department of Economics, A.V.C. College (Autonomous), Mannanpandal, Mayiladuthurai, Tamil Nadu.

** Ph.D. Scholar, Post Graduate and Research Department of Economics, A.V.C. College (Autonomous), Mannanpandal, Mayiladuthurai, Tamila Nadu.

participate fully and directly and take decisions on all issues concerning poverty eradication. Simultaneously, SHGs have the advantage of the assistance be it in terms of credit or technology or market guidance etc., thus reaching the poor faster and more effectively.

Social mobilization is not a spontaneous process; it has to be induced. DRDAs are expected to initiate and sustain the process of social mobilization for poverty eradication by formation, development and strengthening of the Self-Help Groups (SHGs), issues that are key to poverty eradication become entry points for different SHGs depending on the local situation. The groups that are formed with thrift and credit as an entry point have to demonstrate that the poor can secure greater access to credit and other support services for enhancing their income levels.

SELF-HELP GROUPS THROUGH VARIOUS STAGES OF EVOLUTION

Groups Formation

In our society, members are linked by various common bonds like community, blood relation, place of origin, activity, economic status, etc. Therefore, while forming groups, facilitators must recognize the natural bonds and affiliations existing within the society.

Group Stabilization

Through thrift and credit activity amongst the members and building their Group corpus. This provides the members with opportunities to acquire the skills to prioritize scarce resources, to assess the strength of each member, to time the loans and schedule of repay and fix interest rates.

Microfinance

The Group corpus is supplemented with Revolving Fund sanctioned as cash credit limit by the Banks or the group could also have access to credit under the Self-Help Group—Bank Linkage programme of NABARD.

Micro Enterprise Development

Groups takes up Economic activity, of their choice for income generation. All the Groups, particularly Groups formed with the members who are skill less, asset less, destitute and living under abject poverty might not graduate to stage of micro enterprise. Such groups may continue to remain the Micro Finance stage for a longer period of time and may require intensive training and capacity building inputs to enable them to reach higher levels of income generation.

SCOPE OF THE STUDY

The study in question covers working of Self Help Groups at Nagapattinam District, from 2000–2001 to 2004–2005 under the caption "***Working of SHGs at Nagapattinam District***." The researcher has made only chosen coverage by admitting areas like Revolving Fund, Economic Assistance, Infrastructure, Training and Expenditure.

Period of the Study

A period of Five Years starting from 2000–2001 and ending with 2004–2005 has been opted as the period of study.

Objectives of the Study

The principal objectives of the study in question are the following:

1. To analyze the prospect of Revolving Fund of the SHGs in Nagapattinam District.
2. To know about Economic Assistance.
3. To examine the performance of Infrastructure.
4. To go into the details of training on SHGs members, and
5. To bring out the summary of findings of the study.

METHODOLOGY OF THE STUDY

The present study is a case of research work which partly depended on the collection and heavy utilization of the secondary data. The secondary data have been collected from the District Rural Development Agency, Nagapattinam. The objectives framed earlier have been classified, tabulated, analyzed and interpreted using quantitative tools.

NAGAPATTINAM DISTRICT—A PROFILE

Nagapattinam District, the land of communal harmony, was carved out by bifurcating the composite, Thanjavur District on 18.10. 1991. The District has traditionally been referred to East Thanjavur and paddy granary of South India. Nagapattinam District lies on the shores of the Bay of Bengal between Northern Latitude 10.10' and 11.20' East Longitude 79.15' and 79.50'. This peninsular delta District surrounded by Bay of Bengal on the East, Palk strait on the South and land on the west and northern sides. This District is predominantly, a Coastal District having a large coast line of 141 kilometers. This District has a numerous places of historical importance. Nagapattinam is an old port town.

District is having a area of 2715.83 sq. kms in its fold. The District Headquarters is Nagapattinam. The District is enveloping 11 Panchayat Unions, 3 Municipalities, 9 Town

Panchayats on its development side and on the revenue side. It is housing 2 revenue divisions with 4 and 3 taluks respectively and 523 revenue villages.

Nagapattinam is one of the oldest port cities of Chola empire. It was called as "Navel Pattinam"—the city of ships. During 1620 A.D, a Danish settlement was established at Tharangambadi in this District.

DEMOGRAPHIC DETAILS

The growth of the population over the past five decades and the essential characteristics of the population in terms of birth rate, death rate, infant mortality and literacy levels are notable. The marginal farmers (cultivators) and agricultural labours constitute a sizeable population of the labour force in the District. The population of the Nagapattinam District has grown from 4,25,127 in 1951 to 14,88,839 in 2001. The growth rate indicates that there has been a significant increase during 1951–61, the decade with the average growth rate has however stabilized over the past four decades at about 1.65% per annum, according to the 2001 census.

LITERACY LEVEL AMONG THE POPULATION

The literacy level of the Nagapattinam District according to figures available for the year 2001 is 9,96,580 with male literacy level being more that the female literacy level.

DATA ANALYSES AND INTERPRETATIONS ON WORKING OF SHGS AT NAGAPATTINAM DISTRICT, 2000–2001 TO 2004–2005

The secondary data collected in respect of working of SHGs at Nagapattinam District from 2000–2001 to

2004–2005 have been processed involving the due classification and tabulation of the same. The data thus classified have been analyzed and interpreted in regard to the following major heading:

1. Revolving Fund
2. Economic Assistance
3. Infrastructure
4. Training and
5. Expenditure

Revolving Fund Granted by SHGs

The revolving fund is provided to the group to augment the group corpus to enable more number of members to get access to loans and also facilitate increase in the per capita loan available to the members. As the revolving fund becomes part and parcel of the group corps, the groups should follow some norms for utilization as in the case of their saving fund.

Table 1. Revolving Fund

Year	No. of SHGs	Amount (Rs. In Lakhs)
2000–2001	341	34.100
2002–2002	404	40.400
2002–2003	504	50.400
2003–2004	843	84.300
2004–2005	424	42.400
Total	2516	251.600

Source. DRDA, Nagapattinam.

The Table 1 shows Revolving Fund of SHGs in Nagapattinam District that in the year 2000–2001 number of benefitted was 341 out of 2516. Financial assistance rendered to the same, to tune of Rs. 34,100 lakhs SHGs out of the 251.600.

The year 2003–2004 evidenced tremendously a change in the number of self-help groups, *i.e.* 843 and witnessed increased financial assistance to the tune of Rs. 84.300 lakhs. But in the very next year, number of SHGs declined. Hence revolving fund of SHGs also witnessed a fall.

Economic Assistance to the SHGs

Once the SHGs has demonstrated that it has successfully passed through the second stage, it is eligible to receive the assistance for economic activities. This is in the form of loan and subsidy.

Table 2. Economic Assistance to SHGs

Year	No. of SHGs	Amount (Rs. in Lakhs)
2000–2001	62	47.030
2001–2002	95	89.061
2002–2003	11	6.340
2003–2004	226	202.403
2004–2005	153	180.329
Total	547	324.1163

Source. DRDA, Nagapattinam.

The Table 2 reveals the truth that economic assistance to SHGs in Nagapattinam District in the year 2003–2004 was the highest. We are able to witness the highest number of SHGs, *i.e.* 226, were receiving the highest amount of Rs. 202,403 as economic assistance. In contrast, the year 2001–2002 demonstrated the opposite happening.

Infrastructure Facilities to SHGs

Infrastructure fund can be used for strengthening of marketing and related activities.

This Table 3 explains, created infrastructural facilities among the SHGs and the amounts of financial assistance made available to them in the year. The highest level of amount sanctioned in the year 2000–2001 was Rs. 27,944 Lakhs, ever highest. In contrast, the year 2001–2002 exhibited the poor State of affairs prevailing.

Table 3. Infrastructure Facilities Available to SHGs

Year	No. of Work	Amount (Rs. in Lakhs)
2000–2001	8	27.944
2001–2002	2	4.350
2002–2003	—	—
2003–2004	10	17.355
2004–2005	5	24.108
Total	25	73.757

Source. DRDA, Nagapattinam.

Training to SHGs Members

For the identified activities, swarozgaries who need additional skill development/upgradation of skills appropriate training may be identified and suitable training programmes organized. Government institutions like Engineering Colleges, ITIs is Polytechnics, Universities and NGOs may be approached to impart training.

From the table it is identified that the highest amount of Rs. 10,490 lakhs was sanctioned to provide training to 949 SHGs during 2004–05. On the other, the year 2003–2004 demonstrated the lowest of Rs. 3,338 sanctioned to train 1638 SHGs. It is calculated that amount of financial assistance extended to train beneficiaries is nothing to do with the number of beneficiaries really received the training during the period in question.

Table 4. Training to SHGs Members

Year	No. of Members	Amount (Rs. in Lakhs)
2000–2001	200	6.031
2001–2002	1924	8.313
2002–2003	1637	4.100
2003–2004	1638	3.338
2004–2005	949	10.490
Total	6348	32.272

Source. DRDA, Nagapattinam.

Total Expenditure Incurred on SHGs

The expenditure to be borne by the Government will be shared between the State and Centre in the ratio 75 : 25. It should be met out of SGSY funds but should not be included in the individual ceiling applicable to the beneficiary.

Table 5. Total Expenditure on SHGs

Year	Expenditure Incurred (in Rs. lakhs)	Percentage of Achievement
2000–2001	121.885	142.124
2001–2002	142.124	137.19
2002–2003	66.925	48.27
2003–2004	244.896	153.56
2004–2005	257.327	153.56
Total	933.157	645.27

The Table 5 clearly shows that, total expenditure on SHGs incurred year wise and percentage of achievements. The highest expenditure *i.e.*, 344.896 lakhs on SHGs was incurred in the year 2003–2004 which stood for 240.90 of achievement in the same year. The year 2002–2003 showed lowest level of expending to the extent of Rs. 66.925 and represented achievement to the tune of 48.27 percentage.

SUMMARY OF FINDINGS

Swarnjayanti Gram Swarozgar Yojana (SGSY) Scheme helps the poor women through self-help groups. It focuses on organization of the poor at grass roots level through process of social mobilization for poverty eradication. Self-Help Groups have the advantage of the assistance in terms of credit or technology or market guidance etc. Thus SHGs are reacting the poor faster and more effectively.

The SHGs formation works for stabilization, micro finance and micro enterprise development etc. In this way helps to promote economically and socially deprived member of SHGs.

During 2000–2001—2004–2005 the data collected consisted of the revolving fund, economic assistance, infrastructure assistance, total expenditure incurred to provide training to the SHGs members. Hence:

- **(i)** Revolving fund meant for SHGs activities had shown consistent increase in all the years except 2004–05.
- **(ii)** There existed fluctuations in economic assistance to SHGs.
- **(iii)** Infrastructural facilities expenditure increased in the year 2000–2001 compared to the same which was the lowest *i.e.* Rs. 4,350 in 2001–02.
- **(iv)** During the study period, a total 6,348 SHGs received training assistance for which a sum of Rs. 32,272 had spent.
- **(v)** A total of Rs. 933,157 was spent in respect of SHGs during the period of study.

REFERENCES

- Guideline Ministry of Rural Development: ***Swarnjayanti Gram Swarozagar Yojana (SGSY) Government of India,*** New Delhi.
- Nashi S. K. "***Microfinance—A Study of Stree Shakti (SHGs) Programmes,***" Southern Economist, Vol. 43, No. 8 August 15, 2004.
- Chandrakavate, M. S., "***The SHGs Model of Micro Finance. A Silent Movement towards Empowering Rural Women,***" Southern Economist Vol. 44, No. 77, January 1, 2006.

Chapter—5

Socio-Economic Status for Women SHG Members

—*Dr. D. Vengatesan**

—*Dr. Santha Govind***

Women constitute half of the Indian population. Around 80.00 percent of the total female population of India live in rural areas. Out of thirty one million women work force of the country, 20 million are living in rural areas. (The economist intelligence unit, 1977). In India women play a crucial role in agriculture and allied enterprises like dairy and poultry. Training is an important mechanism for transfer of technology and for improve the human resources at all levels. Self-Help Groups are informal groups formed on voluntary basis which are perceived as people institution, providing the poor with the space and support

* Lecturer in Agriculture Extension, Department of Agriculture, Faculty of Agriculture, Annamalai University, Annamalai Nagar, Tamil Nadu.

** Prof. of Agricultural Extension, Department of Agriculture, Faculty of Agriculture, Annamalai University, Annamalai Nagar, Tamil Nadu.

necessary to take effective steps towards greater control on their lives in private as well as in society. Its task stated that SHGs provide the benefits of economics in common action programmes like cost effective credit delivery system promoting democratic culture and Co-operating in programmes with other institution and power to ensure participation (Frenandez, 1995). Research studies showed that the training and participation of women in SHGs made a significant impact on their empowerment, both in social and economic aspects. The present study was undertaken to assess the socio-economic status of SHG members.

METHODOLOGY

The study was conducted during the year 2001 with the Women Self-Help Groups formed by the NGOs under Tamil Nadu Corporation for Development of women of Cuddalore District in Tamil Nadu. They were selected considering the criteria of its establishment period and the location of the NGOs. Past experience and sample literature indicated that, for a group to be developed as SHG, it required a minimum period of 24–36 months, therefore, it was decided to take sample of four years old SHGs only. As on March 2001, there were 60 SHGs which were four years old in the selected blocks. Out of 60 SHGs, it was decided to selected one SHG from each block which had availed maximum loan. Accordingly six Self-Help Groups were selected from six blocks of Cuddalore District. Each SHG consisted of twenty members. Thus six groups comprising 120 women SHG members formed the sample for the study.

The socio-economic status of the members of the SHGs were measured under eleven dimensions for the study. The dimensions selected included educational status, caste, occupational status, family type, family size, farm size, house owned, farm power, livestock possession, material possession and social participation. Based on the responses, simple percentage was calculated. Further, cumulative frequency method was used to categorize the dimensions into three categories *viz.*, low, medium and high categories. Based on the analysis of the individual dimensions, the overall socio-economic status of SHG members was calculated.

FINDINGS AND DISCUSSION

Overall Socio-Economic Status

It is obvious from Table 1, that out of eleven dimensions studied for assessing the overall socio-economic status of Self-Help Group members, 44.17 percent of the women belonged to low level of socio-economic status. About one-third (32.50 percent) and 23.33 percent of the respondents fell under high and medium level of socio-economic status. The low socio-economic status among majority of the respondents may be accounted due to low literacy rate of women in addition to the respondents dependency on agriculture. Further, most of the family possessed less than 2 acres of land. Lack of regular interaction of the group members through periodical meetings and sharing of common problems through requisite trainings from NGOs would be reasons for their low socio-economic

Table 1. Distribution of SHG Members According to their Overall Socio-Economic Status

(*n* = 120)

Category	Number	Percent
Low	53	44.17
Medium	28	23.33
High	39	32.50
Total	120	100.00

status. This result is in consistent with that of Velusamy and Manoharan (1999).

DIMENSION OF SOCIO-ECONOMIC STATUS

This section deals with the results obtained among SHG members with respect to individual dimensions.

It is obvious from Table 2, that out of eleven dimensions studies for assessing the socio-economic status of SHG members, majority of the respondents were illiterate (37.50 percent), belonged to backward caste (54.17 percent), had agriculture as primary occupation (62.50 percent), most of them belonged to nuclear family (67.50 percent) and had maintained family size of upto five members (67.50 percent).

On personal enquiry by the investigator, it was found that most of the women were illiterate, because they got married in their fifteenth or sixteenth years of age itself. The nuclear family system with less members were having sufficient employment potential in rural areas. Most of the SHG members were found to have up to 5 members. Medium level of economy with less amount of income generated from only one enterprise. Could be the probable reason that could be attributed for the majority of the SHGs women to have small size of family. This finding is in line with the findings of Sujatha (1996).

The SHG members' socio-economic status under the dimension of livestock possession was found to be high (48.33 percent). The respondents in this study area had maintained more number of milk animals. The sale of milk continuously gave earnings throughout the year thereby generating additional income. This finding derives support from the findings of Radharani and Laxmidevi (1992).

The respondents fell under medium level category for the rest of the dimensions *viz.,* farm size (56.67 percent), house owned (60.83 percent), farm power (53.33 percent), material

Table 2. Distribution of SHG Members According to their Dimensions of Socio-Economic Status

(*n* = 120)

Dimensions	Category	Number	Percent
Educational Status	Illiterate	45	37.50
	Can Read Only	8	6.67
	Can Read and write	18	15.00
	Primary Level	26	21.67
	Middle Level	13	10.83
	Secondary Level	10	8.33
Caste	Scheduled Caste	55	45.83
	Other Backward Caste	65	54.17
Occupation	Agricultural as Primary Occupation	75	62.50
	Agricultural as Secondary Occupation	45	37.50
Family Type	Nuclear Family	81	67.50
	Joint Family	39	32.50
Family Size	Upto 5 Members	81	67.50
	More than 5 Members	39	32.50
Farm Size	Marginal Farm	25	20.83
	Small Farm	68	56.67
	Big Farm	27	22.50
House Owned	Low	6	5.00
	Medium	73	60.83
	High	41	34.17
Farm Power	Low	27	22.50
	Medium	64	53.33
	High	29	24.17
Livestock Possession	Low	23	19.17
	Medium	39	32.50
	High	58	48.33
Material Possession	Low	12	10.00
	Medium	57	47.50
	High	51	42.50
Social Participation	Low	18	15.00
	Medium	98	81.67
	High	4	3.33

possession (47.50 percent) and social participation (81.67 percent).

This trend may be due to the fact that large farm size would serve as the potential source of income with diverse enterprises. This could generate both supplementary and complementary income for the farm holders. The type of house owned by SHG members differed among the respondents, as most of the sample households possessed land which would have enabled them to replace thatched house with tiles. Normally most of the respondents used bullock which was hired by almost all the farm households for various farm operations. So it may be inferred that most of them fell under medium level of farm power possession.

Majority of them owned cycle, radio, television and grinder. It may be due to the fact that the SHG members were involved in income generating activities such as animal husbandary, poultry keeping, goat rearing and other non-farm activities. The possible reason may be their interest and enthusiasm involved as a result of trainings and other extension activities conducted by NGOs. Velusamy (1996) and Mohanthy (1997) had studied the impact of socio-economic status of women. They have inferred that majority of farm women fell under medium level of socio-economic status. The result of the study is in agreement with this finding.

The overall view of the eleven dimensions showed that most of the dimension fell under low level of socio-economic status. This might be due to the fact that majority of the working rural women are in unorganized sector, where it is difficult to enforce or monitor legal provisions in practice. It is a serious matter that the government itself flouts the law by paying less than the statutory minimum wages for labour. Despite the law on child marriage of girls under 18, it is still common in rural areas, partly because of lack of awareness and the pressure of socially entrenched customs. The status of women in society as individuals in their own rights, has thus consistently been given less importance in all development plans against quantitative targets like income, employment and credit facilities. These are some of the factors affecting SHG women members.

SHG WOMEN AS CHANGE AGENT—A CASE STUDY

T. Kalayankuppam is a small village in Cuddalore District of Tamil Nadu. The inhabitants of the village are mostly labour-turned producers. The low socio-economic status of the women was the major constraint in the expansion of area under cultivation. In this village, water logging in rainy season and water scarcity in summer season, were the factors restricting the expansion of cultivation. This made majority of the women to sustain their living with very low income. Further, the village money lenders and traders exploited this situation. The formal intervention of Tamil Nadu Corporation for Development of Women at T. Kalyankuppam Panchayat happened during this period. The selection of the Panchayat was based on the criteria to identify a village with maximum area with paddy and pulses in Cuddalore district. Tamil Nadu Corporation for Development of Women had undertaken a survey during mid 1996. In the survey, Panchayats with more that 400 farmers was considered as a potential Panchayat. In this way the neighbouring village T. Kalyankuppam was selected during this process.

The task of formation of SHGs in T. Kalyankuppam was assigned to the change agent posted at the site.

Change agent contracted the farm women and explained the details of SHG concept to them. He analyzed the important production problems prevailing among farm women and the ways in which TNCDW was intended to address them. The opportunities in terms of credit, information, technology and marketing by the members through SHG was also brought to their notice in the discussion. However, MNTN (NGOs) officials could not convince women on the practical applicability of the concept. This happened mainly because, as most of them were illiterate, lacked awareness and could not get support from their husbands at the initial period.

Madhar Nala Thondu Niruvanam (NGOs) officials did not become disinterested because of this. They further contracted more farm women belonging to low income category. They explained the purpose of TNCDW to them, showing the opportunity of seeking credit to small and marginal land owned women. He explained to them the way through which their income can be enhanced by formation of SHGs. Expansion of area under cultivation, better technology adoption, collective purchase, group marketing etc., were the few points which were emphasized to them. The presence of an officer at their doorstep, interacting with them in a very informal way was something that enhanced their morale. They assured him all possible assistance and came forward to get involved in the process of Self-Help Group formation. They passed on the information among the other women members of the village. The change agent contracted those women individually at their house and field and created awareness. The women members also persuaded others to join in the group. In this process, no pre-determined membership criteria were followed. Women's interest and willingness to work in the group was the only required criteria. Through this process, 20 members were mobilized within a week.

With the mobilized women, the first meeting at T. Kalyankuppam SHG was conducted. The aim of the meeting was to create awareness and to bring credibility in the process. Change agents along with few more officers from TNCDW and NGOs shared their experience with the women. Clarification of doubts of the farm women was given importance in the meeting. The meeting concluded with a decision to mobilize more women to strengthen the process. After few days the meeting witnessed intensive mobilization activities in the village. More and more women became interested and came forward to join in the SHG. During the first meeting, the preliminary data sheet was filled for getting code number to members. Change agents arranged regular weekly meetings. Considering the high number of women farmers in the SHG, it was suggested to have a lady master farm woman.

The next step of the change agent was to educate the members on the procedure to be followed in conducting various group activities. Change agent first made the members to know about the regular activities of the SHG. The developed norms prevailing in TNCDW were brought to the member's attention. The group members were than asked to discuss and refine the norms to their convenience and interest of the group. The members participation in the process was given prime importance. Thereafter members were educated on the prospects and consequences of the norms. The success and failures of SHGs were taken as examples for this. The process ended with the development of suitable and appropriate mechanism for the execution of the developed norms. The group started maintaining minutes and attendance books.

The next act of change agent was to work for the stabilization of the group activity. The basic leadership strength of the SHG was very weak. This was due to the poor socio-economic condition of the members. There was not improvement in the group stabilization initially. The next act was to make the women increasingly involve in the group maintenance function. Through them, various task like credit-planning, production planning etc., were executed. All these helped in getting the group stabilized within a year from the formal initiation of the process of organization.

The farm women of the village wanted to expand their cultivation. However, the people with land were not ready to lease it out. Their major doubt was about getting rent from the poor women. The animator of the group took up this matter in the SHG meeting. She asked the master farm woman to contact such persons and assure group security. In some cases she also accompanied them. The idea clicked, farm women got land and they also gained confidence in the activity of TNCDW. They also got a feeling of realization of their inherent power and synergetic effect of group.

After this, change agent adopted and educative approach to make the farm women understand their common production problems and causes. The change agent learned the important production problems of the village through farm and home visit. The 'took those problems for discussion in group meetings. Once the members were aware of the existence of the problem and the symptoms, field demonstrations were conducted with emphasis on management aspects. Through subsequent farm and home visits, the change agent further reinforced the understanding of the women.

The initiation of group level collective purchase of inputs was the next activity undertaken by the SHG. The change agent first made the group understand the benefits of the activity and made the group member to gain members. Then the members were asked to find out the various options from the SHGs. The options thus collected were brought and discussed in the meeting. Based on the discussion, the requirement, mechanism and mode of purchase etc., were finalized.

A change in the composition of occupational pattern was observed in accordance with the age of the groups. The dependence of members on wage earning was reduced between group members and non-group members. On the other hand, the women members taking up non-farm activities had increased in the stabilized SHGs.

This was possible mainly due to the training provided by NGOs. The rate of saving per member Rs. from 900 to 1000 per month. The saving was kept under the common fund and lend to members with minimum rate of interest varying from 24 to 36 percent per annum. Income collected as interest, seed money assistance provided by NGOs and credit received from the banks were also pooled with the common fund among the members were the major incentive for better participation. Good repayment performance by the members to bank was also a positive feature. The member of the SHGs in T. Kalayankuppam were actively involved in income generating activities. The enterprise combination of women revealed that as the result of group formation, women were able to diversity their activities through undertaking non-farm and animal husbandry activities.

As a result, the average annual net income of the members was doubled. The SHG members reported that before joining the SHG their net income ranged from 6,000 to 8,000 per year, while the net income during post-group formation had increased from 14,000 to 16,000 per year. Food security and quality of the clothing have also improved. The improvement in the physical quality of life of the group members also significantly contributed for to overall improvement of the life style of the women in T. Kalayankuppam.

The group had lot of plans for the future. The idea of developing farm women Clubs comprising of women folk of the SHG members to prepare value added products from various crops and raw materials, thus utilizing the spare time of women folk was one of the major plan. This can stabilize the income of women in times of off-season. Thus looking into the process of empowerment of the SHG members in total, it could be inferred that the empowerment reached from all these activities has made a feeling of secure among the members to maintain the group even in the absence of Tamil Nadu Corporation for Development of Women and Madhar Nala Thondu Niruvanam (NGOs).

CONCLUSION

Among the eleven dimensions considered for calculating the socio-economic status, it was inferred that only the dimensions *viz.*, livestock possession, house owned, material possession, farm power and farm size the respondents were found under medium to high level category. Hence, efforts to improve these dimensions uniformly among SHG members should be taken up by the sponsoring agencies.

REFERENCES

- Fernandez, A. P. ***Self-Help Groups—The Concept***, Mysore Rehabilitation Development Agency: 1–15.
- Mohanthy, M. 1997. "***Decision-Making in Home and Farm Related Activities***," Kurushetra, 43(11) : 30–37.
- Radharani, N. and A. Laxmidevi. 1992. "***Problems of Biogas Beneficiaries***," Indian Journal of Extension Education, 28 (3 and 4) : 44–48.
- Sujatha, Jane, J. 1996. ***Gender Analysis in different Farming Systems***, Unpublished Ph.D. Thesis, Tamil Nadu Agricultural University, Coimbatore.
- Velusamy, R. 1996. ***Impact of Non-governmental Organization in Rural Development***, Unpublished M.Sc. (Ag.) Thesis, Tamil Nadu Agricultural University, Madurai.
- Velusamy, R. and M. Manoharan, 1999. "***Characteristics of Beneficiaries of NGOs According to Gender***," Journal of Extension Education, 10 (1) : (55–57)

Chapter—6

Self-Help Groups: At The Cross-Roads

—*Dr. M. Hilaria Soundari**

> *"If India is not to perish, we have to begin with the lowest rung of the ladder, if that was rotten, all work done at the top or the intermediate rungs was bound ultimately to fall"*
>
> **—Mahatma Gandhi**

At the threshold of the third millennium, India has remarkably in multiple phases of life. Its progress in the field of information technology, bio-technology and nano-technology are significant. However, according to Census 2001, 72.2% of the Indian population is in rural area. Among them, 34.7% of the poorest population (the population that lives on 3/4 of the poverty line or less) still lives on less than

* Lecturer in Applied Research, Department of Applied Research Gandhigram Rural Institute (Deemed University), Gandhigram, Dindigul District Tamil Nadu.

US$1 a day and 79.9% live on US$2 per day (*Mehta* and *Shah*, 2002). Most of them are deprived of the basic amenities. They are in need of basic requirements of Physical, Knowledge, Electronic and Economic connectivity (*Kalam*, 2003). To uplift the people below poverty line and to provide basic amenities are the major concern of the Indian Government. To reach out these rural mass an effective approach like Self-Help Groups (SHGs) was considered as inevitable.

SHGs FOR WOMEN

Women of India in all spheres of life silently or stridently spelt out their suppressed and dehumanized existence. The disparity was manifested in various forms, the most obvious being the trend of female ratio *i.e.*, 933 in the population (Census Report, 2001). According to UNDP—Human Development Report (HDR) 1997 gender disparity can be seen through the lens of the gender-related development index (GDI) and gender empowerment measure (GEM). In this HDR, India's GDI rank is 70 and GEM rank is 86 out of 94 countries. Consequently in the Ninth Plan (1997–2002) the Indian Government in its welfare programs shifted the concept of development to empowerment. The approach widely adopted to achieve this goal of empowerment women was widely accepted as 'Self-Help Groups' in 2001.

Thus to reach out rural poor and neglected women it was essential to have various programmes. SHGs have emerged as a vital approach. It has plunged into the nuke and corner of Indian rural hamlets.

EMERGENCE OF SHGs

Muhammad Yunus (1976) of Chittagong University in Bangladesh introduced this popular approach of

Self-Help Group (SHG). The concept of 'Nijeri Kori' (which means literally 'we do it ourselves' or self-help) for poor women to start small business through Grameen Bank was his initial step. Now the bank has more than 1000 branches and 12,000 workers and a saving fund of $32.92 million. The Self-Help Group movement became silent a revolution within a short span in the rural credit delivery system in many parts of the world. It has been documented that nearly 53 developing countries including India, have taken up this on a large scale. Viewing Self-Help Groups as an effective welfare programme in Ninth Five Year Plan (1997–2002) the Indian Government adopted this approach to uplift the rural poor. National programmes like Support to Training and Employment Programme (STEP), Training Cum-Production Centers (NORAD), Rashtriya Mahila Kosh (RMK), Indira Mahila Yojana (IMY), etc. also focus on promoting SHGs.

Concept of SHGs

'Self-Help Groups were voluntary small group structures for mutual aid in the accomplishment of a specific purpose. They were usually formed by peers who had come together for mutual assistance in satisfying a common need, overcoming a common handicap or life-disrupting problem, and bringing about desired change' (***Katz*** and ***Bender***, 1976). According to the Tamil Nadu Corporation for Development of Women (1999) Self-Help Groups were small, economically homogeneous and affinity groups of rural or urban poor, voluntarily formed to save and contribute to a common fund to be lent to its members as per group decision and for working together for social and economic uplift of their families and community.

Rural Coverage

SHGs have been a forum where the rural women are able to come together and strive towards the common well-being. While many of the welfare programmes have failed to get the participation and involvement of the rural women, SHGs have ensured their enhanced participation. In Tamil Nadu, SHGs were officially picked up its momentum in 1997. At present there are more than 616 NGOs working as a Government approved agencies to organize the rural poor women. Their major focus are capacity building, social and economic empowerment. In August 2004, there were 1,78,000 SHGs with 29,84,000 women members and average savings of these groups are Rs. 531.96 crores (***Mutram***, Oct 2004). While completing a decade, SHGs have to be analyzed radically and take right direction for the further progress and development.

IMPORTANT FUNCTIONS OF SHGs

Government had designed a variety of measures to reach the poor women with SHGs. The innovative SHGs have become one of successful measure of the recent past. It focuses on building human, financial and organization capacity. It—

- Helps women to achieve social/critical awareness of each individual, leading to the realization of their need for unity, dignity, mutual respect, education and cooperative enterprise;
- Fosters organizational ability in economic enterprises with an in-built sense of belonging and identity as a functional group;
- Mobilizes working capital, initially by treating regular thrift and savings as their first expense and not as a surplus of income over expenditure;
- Strives to be an autonomous and self-regulated body through peer pressure, flexibility, concern and responsiveness;
- Develops systems that are simple to assimilate, slowly upgrading, accepting increased responsibilities in all management roles;

- Emerges as pressure groups to realize their dues and rights from the Government;
- Responds to the emerging needs, design and develop new products in savings, credit, entrepreneurial support, consultancy, training, technology ingression, etc.

Central Government's Swaranjayanti Gram Swarojgar Yojana (SGSY) and State Government's Tamil Nadu Corporation for Development of Women (Mahalir Thittam) focuses on the same purpose.

TREND OF SHGs

(a) *Conducive Elements.* SHGs have made women to move out of their home limits. It had given them the courage to contact and confront the officials. With the limited functional literacy they have gained the skill of maintaining accounts and registers. Many of them have undergone various training programmes and it has given them the self-confidence to be entrepreneurs. The impressive performances of SHG women have drawn more number of NGOs and GOs to be in the fray to form SHGs. Both the State and Central Governments have come forward to channelize the schemes through SHGs.

NGOs, Government machineries, educational institutions, Commercial Banks and corporate sectors have acknowledged SHGs to be an effective body of implementing the divergent programmes. Invariably they are convinced that SHGs are one of the feasible modes to organize the people at the grassroot. Though the formation of SHGs is accepted as an essential element of people's growth and development still there are large numbers of remote villages and under served hamlets that are left without being touched by the SHG movement. These could be accessed at the course of time.

(b) *Constraining Elements.* There are high competitions among the NGOs in covering more number of hamlets. False promises and instant loans with high interest are given lavishly to attract the people. Consequently, the civic consciousness and sense of social responsibility among the mushrooming groups are demoralized.

Convergence of services of key line departments of Government like health, agriculture, police, education, animal husbandry, fisheries, etc., with SHGs may provide a wider scope. But it can reduce the significance of SHGs in the major platforms decision-making and policy decisions. Each department claims that SHGs are under their purview but seldom anybody cares to take care of their needs and problems.

While strengthening Cluster Level Federations (CLFs) it is essential to consider the caste and class factors that dominate the Indian society. Even the continuous training and exposure programmes have brought them together in a subtle way. The dominance of caste group may continue and the poor Dalits may be neglected.

PLIGHT OF THE LESS PRIVILEGED

The mission statement of the Tamil Nadu Corporation for Development of Women (TNCDW) wishes to build capacity of poor and disadvantaged Dalit women in order that they are enabled to cross all social and economic barriers. But in reality there are numerous problems faced in reaching out the less privileged. Among Dalits so far only 49% of them could be covered in this programme. Some of them are—

— Most of the NGOs are still hesitant to reach out the Dalit hamlets with fear of facing rejection from the caste people of the village.

— Largely the NGO workers or Government officials are non-dalits who could not enter into the shoe of the Dalits to comprehend their difficulties.

— From the NGOs perception the time and energy to be spent to form the Dalit groups are doubled. For they are unprepared to receive any NGOs with the fear of being cheated.
— It is also said that some of the NGOs collect high interest for the loans.
— Many of them are unable to avail the subsidy loans. Because they are not able to spend money to get the community certificate which is a mandatory to get it.
— The attitude and outlook of the bank officials are not very positive towards the poor people as they are not sure of their repayment.
— Most of the Dalit people are below poverty line, it is an added risk of making them do the repayment of loan.
— Their capacity to retain the assets created from the loans are limited as they have negligible resorts for any emergencies.
— When the Dalits succeed with certain pioneering work, they are highly criticized by the caste people of the village. They are sarcastically commented for going out of the village too.
— Concerning Tribals still many of the hamlets are untouched as they have either limited or no transport facilities.

Discriminated Treatment for Women

TNCDW has resolved to reach out to women living below poverty line. It aims to promote and ensure the human rights of women at all stages of their life cycle, to advocate changes in Government policies and programmes in favor of disadvantaged women and to empower women to work together with men as equal partners and to work together for equality, sustainable development, and communal harmony.

But in reality, as a controversial portrayal of Tamil Nadu Corporation for Women of Development men largely occupy officials' seats. The rural women who enter the offices for the first time feel much reluctance to articulate their difficulties to them. The achievement of equal status of poor women as participants, decision makers and beneficiaries in the democratic, economic, social and cultural spheres of life through SHGs is insisted. But in the wider scenario the passing of women's bill in the Parliament is still at stake.

ILLITERACY AMONG WOMEN

Promotion of entrepreneurship amongst SHG members is vital. Literacy is the prime concern of the rural poor. It restricts their entrepreneur venture. Entrepreneurship also requires accounting, marketing and managerial skill. It has become difficult for the poor illiterate women to cope with these demands. Sustainability through conscious promotion of self-monitoring, self-reliance and independent functioning of SHGs is an appreciable effort. According an empirical study (***Soundari***, 2003), the illiteracy rate of Dalit women in Dindigul District was 77%. Hence it becomes difficult to make them as sustainable body. Consistent training and skill development practice has to be offered to them. The gender gap in literacy has to be bridged at the course of time.

Literacy Rates (%) in India (1951–2001)

Census Year	Persons	Males	Females	Male-Female gap in Literacy Rate
1951	18.33	27.16	8.86	18.30
1961	28.30	40.40	15.35	25.05
1971	34.45	45.96	21.97	23.98
1981	43.57	56.38	29.76	26.62
1991	52.21	64.13	39.29	24.84
2001	65.38	75.85	54.16	21.70

AT THE CROSS-ROAD

SHG is a path that leads to prosperity. Just being a SHG member does not decide anybody's fate. But the direction in which the SHG moves need to determine the destiny of the members. In this path, the intense training and analytical skills given to the women enable them to choose the better direction. Their move may be accompanied by significant others for a limited time. They can show the best of the direction, but it is ultimately the group, which can decide about the direction. The intense involvements with the SHG members have shown the possible four directions that a group can take. They are being discussed below:

Directions of SHGs

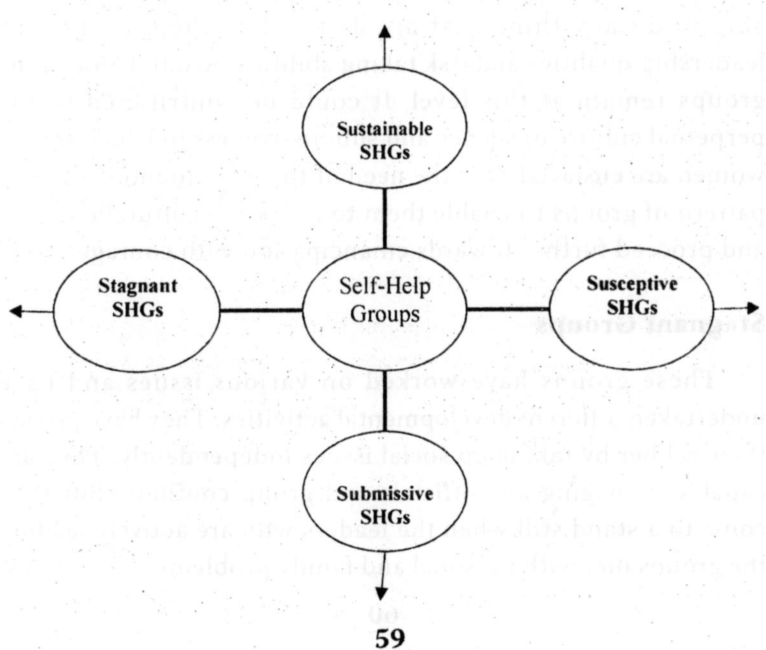

Susceptible Groups

If the groups are completely focus only on loan and economic benefits, they cannot often draw line between them and the pawnbrokers. The groups tend to meet the end as soon as its needs are met. Unnecessary quarrels and conflicts creep in on account of money. Impatience and intolerance among these members are prominent. Some of the leaders or members tend to cheat them. They get dissolved when meager problems arises. Studies have shown that around 10% of the SHGs get dissolved. Most of them takes place from three months to two years.

Submissive Groups

Some of the groups even after six to ten years continue to exist but they continue to depend on others. They are regular in attending training programmes and other meetings. Dependency syndrome is the major drawback of this category of groups. They need GOs or NGOs to back them up for every activity. They are able to do any thing that are dictated to them. They lack leadership qualities and risk taking abilities. Around 55% of the groups remain at this level. It could be contributed to the perpetual culture of silence and submissiveness to which Indian women are enslaved. It is the need of the hour to intervene this pattern of groups to enable them to break the cultural clutches and proceed further towards emancipation with courage.

Stagnant Groups

These groups have worked on various issues and have undertaken different developmental activities. They have proved their caliber by taking up social issues independently. They are capable managing any officials and group conflicts. But they come to a stand still when the leaders who are actively leading the groups met with personal and family problems. The groups' dynamic undertaking comes to a stand stili. They lack secondary level leaders who can take the groups further. With the change of active leaders they may be able change the facet of the group. Around 20% of the SHGs come under the stagnant groups.

Sustainable Groups

SHGs that have learnt the art of interdependence have shown significant growth. The members develop good relationship and confidence among them. They take up group entrepreneur activities. The new successful ventures boost the morale of the group. Even when the existing pattern of SHGs terminates its way of functioning they will be able to proceed. For instance, there is group named Vidiyal SHG in Lakshmipuram village near Vathalagundu. This group of women has got the revolving fund and economic activity loan. The highest educational level of the group is only V standard. But they have made use of all the training programmes to develop the skills. They made use of the opportunity to express the basic needs of the village in the Grama Shabha meetings. Whenever need arouse they also met the District Collector, Bank Officials and other Government machineries. With the help of the economic activity, they not only bought milk animals but also started the cooperative milk society with the tie up of Aavin.

Their growth has been reflected in the growth of the village by getting the basic amenities. Their awareness have created the first generation in higher education. Their civic consciousness has helped them to come out the caste bondages of oppression. They have proved themselves to be successful Panchayat Ward Members. They have become the dynamic entrepreneurs and managers in administering the cooperative society. They have become the source of inspiration for other women to join SHGs. The present status of the group reveals that they can march forward whether any other supportive forces are present or not. They have become sustainable in their progress.

CONCLUSION

Women's emancipation can be reflected with the promotion of large number of sustainable SHGs. It can ensure the increased participation of women in SHGs. It can provide conducive environment in groups where women demand knowledge and information, empowering themselves to change their lives. It can challenge the oppressive structure of the society. Such SHGs can be created more among rural areas where disparity persists with uncompromising tenacity and among the disadvantaged communities. If so, SHGs cannot only enhance the national conscience but also enable in achieving Millennium Development Goals.

"Development if not engendered is indeed endangered"

—UNFPA India report 1997

REFERENCES

- Katz, Alfred. H and Bender, Eugene. I, ***The Strength in US: Self-Help Groups in the Modern World—New Viewpoints,*** New York: Franklin Watts, 1976, p. 6.
- Mehta, Aasha; Shah, Amita (2002). ***Chronic Poverty in India: Overview Study.*** Chronic Poverty Research Centre. Retrieved on 2006–07–24.
- Mutram, TNCDW, Chennai, Oct., 2004.
- Srinivasan, K., ***India: Towards Population and Development Goals.*** (UNFPA) New Delhi: Oxford University Press, 1997.
- TNCDW, Credit Guidelines for SHGs. Chennai, 1999.
- http://orissagov.nic.in/panchayat/pura.asp
- http://en.wikipedia.org/wiki/Demographics_of_India
- http://presidentofindia.nic.in/scripts/sllatest1.jsp?id=107
- http://www.tamilnaduwomen.org/

Part—II

Women Empowerment : Proactive Role of SHGs

Part—II

Women Empowerment : Proactive Role of SHGs

Chapter—7

Gender Economics, Women Empowerment and Self-Help Groups

—Dr. A. Ramalingam*

RETHINKING ECONOMICS THROUGH FEMINIST APPROACH

The feminist analysis distinguishes between gender and sex: The gender distinction (Masculine/ Feminine dualism) is socially constructed rather than biologically determined.

The feminist analysis focuses on the current neglect of gender dimensions of human economic behaviour:

The 'classroom climate'—including the pedagogy, the pattern of interaction with men and women students, sexist assumptions and sex stereotyping in textbooks—may make women students less confident about succeeding in analytical, critical and creative economic thinking.

* Reader in Economics, Post Graduate and Research Department of Economics, A.V.C. College (Autonomous), Mannanpandal, Mayiladuthurai, Tamil Nadu.

Recent feminist theory questions many of the basic assumptions and values of mainstream economics. The distinguishing characteristic of mainstream economics is the assumption of (men's autonomous self interested behaviour) 'homo economicus' (economic man) in contrast to "Femina economica" (women's connected, other interested behaviour). The feminist critique of mainstream economics focuses on the asymmetry in the social domain.

ASYMMETRY IN THE SOCIAL DOMAIN

Separative spheres for men and women *i.e.*, Male Super Ordination and Female subordination determine the social functioning of humans. Autonomous, rational, detached–masculine projection prevails in contrast to dependent, emotional, connected feminine projection. What is needed is a conception of "human" behaviour that does not confuse gender with sex. Feminist economists have challenged mainstream economics as ***raceless or genderless economics***. Feminists attack the neoclassical model of the detached, ***rational maximiser***.

Families as institutions receive almost no attention in traditional economics. Women and children are neither heard nor seen. As observed by Amartya Sen, "In the standard theory of prices and equilibrium individuals and firms are visible but definitely no families."

Traditional economic perspective contributes nothing to an understanding of caring services.

Empirical studies cast great doubt on the relevance of the ***neoclassical assumptions of rationality, homogeneity and equal opportunity***.

Models of perfect competition do not explain economic discriminations, which are related to race ethnicity and gender differentials. The paradigm of perfect competition does not offer an adequate explanation of economic asymmetries (in Marxian term "exploitation").

Several decades have passed since imperfect competition has been recognised as a characteristic of economic society. Yet economists continue to focus on perfect markets in which labour is homogenous, people are rational decision makers and economic maximisers (maximisers of material gain) and all individuals enjoy equal opportunity and freedom of choice in economic activity.

Gender disparities contribute to differentials in power — the power of property, access and influence—also under endowment, under utilization and under-performance and under rewarding.

Neoclassical economics is not a multicultural economics—rarely employs an explicit concept of power/powerlessness. Instead neoclassical theory prefers the language of endowments and preferences of individuals. Neoclassical economics explains differences in rewards as due to differences in marginal productivities.

MODELS OF GENDER DISCRIMINATION

Economists who have explored richer models of feminist economic behaviour include:

Gary Becker, 1957, 1972
Jacob Mincer, 1962
George Stigler, 1968
Easter Boserup, 1970
Steven Salop and Josep Stiglitz, 1977
L. Beneria, 1982
Amartya Sen, 1985,1992
Barbara Bergmann, 1986
Robert H. Frank, 1988
George A. Akerlof and

Janet L. Yellen, 1988
Claudia Dale Goldwin, 1990
Jean Shackelford, 1992
Nancy Folbre, 1994
Bina Agarwal, 1994 and Julie A. Nelson 1992, 93, 95

The examination of the basis of gender division has been the focus of recent works by feminist economists.

Concept of Gender

"Gender" has now become one of the busiest, most restless terms in the English language. The term gender is used indiscriminately to describe different things at different times. Sometimes it means 'women', sometimes 'sex'. Of late, much insistence is made to define gender precisely. Gender refers not to men and women, but to relationship between them and to the ways in which the roles of women and men, girls and boys are socially constructed." (Common Wealth Plan of Action and Gender Development 1995).

Gender draws attention to the artificiality of the behaviour of women and men. Gender generates the social division between sexes and places both men and women as "mutually exclusive categories." Gender is an arbitrary discrimination, institutionally constituted firmly, which need an intense analysis to deconstruct them.

Sex vs. Gender

'Gender' as an analytical term is different from 'sex'. Sex is a physical distinction; gender is social and cultural. The sex of an individual is biologically determined, whereas gender characterises—masculinity and femininity—are socially constructed a product of nurturing, conditioning, and socio-cultural norms and expectations and these characteristics change over time.

Sex is defined as the biological dichotomy between female and male, chromosomally determined, and for the most part, unalterable, while gender is refered to the well determined cultural symbols, normative concepts, institutional structure and internalised self-images.

Masculinity and femininity form an edifice of attitudes and assumptions, behaviours and activities differentially marked for women and men. The disturbing fact is that masculinity and femininity are not independent categories but form a hierarchical relation, resulting in gender inequality.

GENDER INEQUALITY

Gender inequalities impose costs in terms of lower output, lower development of human resource capacities, and lower levels of leisure and well being. Gender inequality also reduces the productivity of the next generation. The probability of children being enrolled in school increases with their mother's educational level, and extra income going to mothers has a more positive impact on household investment in nutrition, health and education of children than extra income going to fathers (World Bank, 1995).

Gender inequality is therefore economically inefficient.

The Family in Economic Theory

The family is a black box for most economists.

A wide range of assumptions is rooted implicitly or explicitly in both economic theory and economic policy about:

- how family members interact
- take decisions and share resources
- the motivations that guide their actions and the likely outcomes for their welfare and productivity
- assumptions regarding intra-family motivations and behaviour.

Implications of incorrect assumptions about family relations affect the efficiency and welfare impact of public programmes. The existing definitions and assumptions about family relations—especially gender relations—are all fallacious and policies formulated on this basis reinforce existing male privilege.

In economic theory two types of models of the family household predominate:

(i) ***The Unitary Model*** (Neoclassical model) outlined most explicitly by Gary Becker; this model is implicit in much of economic theory and policy.

(ii) ***The Bargaining Model*** (Marxist model) outlined as the more realistic alterative by a number of economists in recent years.

The unitary model treats the household as a single entity in relation to both consumption and production. It assumes that all household resources and incomes are pooled.

Resource allocation within the household is explained by assuming an ***altruistic household head*** who represents the household's tastes and preferences and seeks to maximize household utility (Becker 1965, 1981); or

By assuming that ***all household members share the common preferences and interests*** (Samuelson, 1956).

In recent years, every assumption of ***the unitary model has been challenged on empirical grounds***:

- assumptions of shared preferences and interests
- pooled incomes, and
- altruism as the guiding principle of intra-household allocations.

Alternative Bargaining models characterize household decision making as some form of 'bargaining' (Models by Manser and Brown, 1980; McElroy and Honey, 1981; and Jones, 1983).

The bargaining models use the game theoretic approach to incorporate the complex aspects of the family decision making process.

— These models recognize individual self-interest as a central component of intra-family interactions.
— They also allow for individual differences in preferences, in budget constraints, in control over resource use, etc.,
— They can accommodate ***gender asymmetries***—can understand the full complexity of gender relations and their outcomes.

In the bargaining model, intra-household interaction is characterized as containing elements of both co-operation and conflict.

The outcome of intra-household allocation of resources, tasks and so on depends on the relative bargaining power of the household members (Bina Agarwal, 1997).

Both gender and age can affect bargaining power. Women in relation to men and children in relation to adults typically have lower bargaining power.

The characterisation of the family/household impinges not just academic analysis but also critically on policy analysis—*i.e.* the unitary conceptualisation of the family in Indian context—ceilings legislations. In India, legislative definitions and assumption have policy implications, *e.g.*, definition of family in Land Ceiling Laws of States. Family unit is defined as including cultivator, spouse, minor sons, and unmarried minor daughters. With the exception of few States, unmarried adult daughters receive no recognition at all. They form neither as part of the family unit nor as separate units. Adult sons are treated as separate units.

In unitary model of household, the resources are directed to male household heads (adult males), assuming equitable intra-household sharing of benefits, and an efficient allocation of resources and tasks.

Bargaining model suggests that the transfer of resources to men, would reduce the bargaining power of women and increase inequalities in the intra-household allocations of productive resources and consumption goods, leading to lower productivity gains for women.

The welfare, efficiency, and equity implications differ by gender in case of intra–household allocations.

A bargaining model would take account of gender dimensions and ***would direct policy interventions*** towards legal and institutional changes.

In India, the most explicit definitions of a family are found in land reform legislations and are implicitly seen in many legal and other provisions, such as inheritance laws, social security schemes, judicial rulings, and so on.

The following views of intra-family gender relations are indicated in legislative definitions: (B. Agarwal, 2002)

- Men are the natural heads of households and share the resources equitably for the welfare of all household members;
- Men are the appropriate representatives of family in public decision making forums;
- Men are primary producers and thus the legitimate claimants to productive resources such as land.
- Women are largely dependents and this dependence status is unproblematic, even desirable. Women are expected to rely on one or other male relative (father, husband, or son) as the case may be for their entire lives.
- Marriage is typically universal and stable (Bina Agarwal, 2002).

Gender Discrimination: Male Superordination/Female Subordination

Gender Ideology:

Sphere	Type
Education:	Girls may be sent to local schools.
Skills:	Girls may be encouraged to acquire home-oriented skills with little market value (cooking)
Health:	Girls may be given inferior nutritional intake; Differential maternal care for female and male children; Medical attention may be delayed in case of females.
Employment:	Soft Jobs even in professions (social welfare, cultural sphere); Wage and technology differentiation; Females may be largely concentrated in contractual and unorganised sector works.
Placements:	Men as productive earners, women as supplementary earners.
Property:	Females may be denied a share in inheritance of parental property and assets. (Negligible access to property income)
Atrocities:	Differential access to food, education and medical care, dowry death, rape, wife beating, sexual harassment, forced prostitution, sexual abuse in work place, abuse of widows. Female

	infanticide, female foeticide, sex-selective abortion, coerced pregnancy, child marriage, genital mutilation, child labour, etc.
Domestic violence:	1. at natal home 2. at conjugal home. Physical abuse, Sexual abuse, emotional, verbal and psychological abuse, economic abuse, intimidation and harassment.

GENDER JUSTICE AND GENDER EQUALITY

Constitutional & Legal Rights of Women in India

Fundamental Rights

Article 14	— Equality before law
Article 15	— Prohibition of discrimination on grounds of inter-alia, sex
Article 15(3)	— To make special provisions for women and children
Article 16	— Equality of opportunity in public employment

Directive Principles

Article 39(a)	— To secure for all citizens, men and women equally, right to means of livelihood
Article 39(c)	— Equal pay for equal work
Article 42	— Just and human conditions of work and maternity relief

Fundamental Duties

Article 51 A (e) — To renounce practices derogatory to the dignity of women.

Relevant Indian Laws Relating to Women

The Hindu Marriage Act, 1955

The Special Marriage Act, 1954

The Hindu Succession Act, 1956

The Hindu Adoption and Maintenance Act, 1956

The Child Marriage Restraint (Amendment) Act, 1976

The Factories Act, 1948: Mines Act, 1952 and Plantation Labour Act, 1951

The Employees State Insurance Act, 1948

The Maternity Benefits Act, 1961

The Factories (Amendment) Act, 1976

The Equal Remuneration Act, 1976

The Contract Labour (Regulation and Abolition) Act, 1978

The Dowry Prohibition Act, 1961

The Immoral Traffic (Prevention) Act, 1986

Amendment to the Criminal Laws, 1983

Family Courts Act, 1984

Indecent Representation of Women (Prohibition) Act, 1986

The Commission of Sati (Prevention) Act, 1987

The National Commission for Women Act, 1992

Tamil Nadu Prohibition of Eve Teasing Act, 1997

Protection of Women from Domestic Violence (Against Women) Act, 2005

Indian Panel Code, 1860

Code of Criminal Procedure, 1973

Indian Evidence Act, 1872

Equal Rumuneration Act, 1976

The Muslim Women (Protection Right on Divocrce) Act, 1986.

The legal position thus effectively affirms and promotes the principles of equity and equality of women and takes care of their special needs.

GENDER DIVIDE IN INDIAN CONTEXT AND WOMEN'S ECONOMIC EMPOWERMENT

The concept of gender gap is highly relevant in the Indian context where gender based prejudices at both social and economic levels abound. The acknowledgement of gender discrimination is important because development takes place within the context of a given socio-economic framework where women are treated unequally. Hence, their responses and relations to the decision-making process are not congruent across the gender divide. Discrimination has a number of negative implications in the context of a developing country, which results in low female participation, high fertility, reduces efficiency and slows down economic growth.

Women 'alienation' refers to powerlessness, normlessness and social isolation. 'Alienation' is not merely a concept but a perspective which can very well serve to comprehend the human conditions in its dehumanised form. Women experiences alienation mainly as powerlessness as evidenced by her loss of control over the essential conditions of her working life.

Women 'empowerment' looks at basic human rights and attempts at organizing to attain them. Social action groups have used the term 'empowerment' variously and often loosely in academic writing and across the world. In the present context 'empowerment' could be defined as "a process that enhances the ability of disadvantaged ('powerless') individuals or groups to challenge and change (in their favour) existing power relationships that place them in subordinate economic, social, and political positions."

Empowerment can manifest itself in acts of individual resistance as well as in group mobilization. From the institutional perspective empowerment is the process of setting the right environment and structure as well as creating circumstances in which people can use their faculties and abilities to fully actualise their potential. 'Economic empowerment' involves the ability of women to engage in income generating activities, which will give them an independent income, since financial dependence is one of the key sources of subordination of women. Entitling women with land would, on the one hand, empower them economically, and on the other hand, strengthen their ability to challenge social and political gender inequalities. That is, land rights would enhance women's "freedom to achieve" or capability to function in non-economic spheres as well. Women may be provided with educational opportunities, especially with access to the frontier areas. Knowledge and skills, which will give them, access to well-paid and high profile jobs. Women also need to be given leadership training which includes activities in which a women can take a stand, gather support and push for something, and be recognized as a participant in this struggle. A women needs to be able to identify and address the factors, which affect women directly and differently. Women's empowerment can positively influence the lives not only of women themselves but also of men, and of course those of children.

The empowerment value of basic education is so obvious. Gender bias is reduced by an expansion of female literacy. Female literacy is a considerable force in reducing fertility. Female literacy and female labour-force participation have a negative effect on fertility. Female education can be expected to reduce desired family size for several reasons: First, educated women are more likely to voice resentment against the burden of repeated pregnancies and to take action to lighten that burden. Second, educated women are likely to be less dependent on their sons as a source of social status and old-age security and this too may lead to some reduction in desired family size. Third, educated women often have higher aspirations for their children, combined with lower expectations from them in terms of labour services provided. Fourth, the opportunity cost of time tends to be comparatively high for educated women, and this creates an incentive to minimize such time-intensive activities as child-bearing and child-rearing.

These factors imply a negative association between female education and desired family size. Greater literacy and educational achievements of disadvantaged groups can increase their ability to resist oppression, to organise politically, and to get a fair deal.

MICRO FINANCE INNOVATIONS IN ECONOMIC EMPOWERMENT

Cutting across all approaches, women's micro-credit groups are now proliferating throughout India. Supported by government policy and NGO interventions, these are being seen as a magic wand for all the ills of development. For the poor, whose only other alternative source of support may be the ubiquitous moneylender, middleman or middle woman, self help groups (SHGs) serve as respectable alternative. The concept of micro finance was introduced in India in 1992 for over coming the existing constraints and providing adequate credit to the poor in general and the weaker section in particular by following a simple procedure. The system of micro finance has several merits such as near cent percent recovery, low transaction cost, easy monitoring and less time consuming. The SHGs availing micro finance, have shown an excellent record of loan repayment, as the amount repaid is recycled for giving fresh loan to the same or new members, the beneficiaries develop a sense of involvement. Members of the group feel that the repayment is made to their own group and not to any outside agency.

Micro finance institutions (mFIs) are those, which provide thrift, credit and other financial services and products for the poor in rural, semi-urban or urban areas for enabling them to raise their income levels and improve living standards. Micro finance institutions and Self-Help Groups are important vehicles for credit delivery to self-employed persons, particularly, women in rural and semi-urban areas. Issues relating to the structure and sustainability, funding, regulations and capacity building for micro finance delivery are engaging the attention of the Reserve Bank of India. The failure of the "trickle down" model has caused concern and has set many people thinking about the very meaning of development, the new concern has been reinforced by a few evolving trends. Hence, the search for a viable alternative strategy has become a matter of urgent necessity.

SHGs: ALTERNATIVE CATALYST OF DEVELOPMENT

A SHG is a registered or unregistered group of micro entrepreneurs with a homogeneous social and economic background voluntarily coming together to save small amounts regularly and multiply agreeing to contribute to a common fund to meet their emergency needs on mutual help basis. The group members use collective wisdom and peer pressure to ensure proper end—use of credit and timely repayment thereof. SHGs interventions in rural development provide people's participation. Indeed, development is a process of mutual endeavour, which calls for the participation of all segments of society. This can be summed-up by a slogan:

"One for all, all for one and all for all"

REFERENCES

- Amartya Sen. ***Resources, Values and Development***, Oxford, 1984, 1999.
- Bina Agarwal, ***A Field of One's Own***, Cambridge University Press, New York, 1994 (New Delhi, 1998).
- Bina Agarwal in Rakesh Mohan, ed. ***Facets of the Indian Economy***, Oxford, 2002.
- Jaya Indiresan, ***Education for Women Empowerment***, Delhi, Konark Publishers Pvt Ltd, 2002.
- Jean Dreze and Amartya Sen, INDIA ***Economic Development and Social Opportunity***, New Delhi, 1999.
- Ravishankar Kumar Singh, ***Role of NGOs in Socio-Economic Development***, Delhi, Abhijeet Publications, 2003.
- Reserve Bank of India, ***Report on Trend and Progress of Banking in India*** 1999–2000, December, 2000.
- Reserve Bank of In0dia 2002–03, September 2003.

Chapter—8

Empowerment of Women through SHGs in Madurai District—An Empirical Analysis

—Dr. R. Haridoss*
—J. Fredrick**

INTRODUCTION

Women represent fifty percent of population, make up thirty percent of the official labour force, perform sixty percent of all working hours, receive ten percent of the world income and own less than one percent of the world property. They share multiple responsibilities and perform important roles as producers of food, managers of natural resources, earners of income and caretakers of household affairs. Moreover, they are the active agents of change and the dynamic promoters of social transformation playing a vital role in shaping the destiny of future

* Prof. and Head, Department of Mathematical Economics, School of Economics, Madurai Kamaraj University, Madurai, Tamil Nadu.
** Lecturer in Economics, Department of Economics, N.M.S.S. Vellaichamy Nadar College, Madurai.

generations. Yet in the gendered social formations they are placed below the hierarchy of men.

Empowerment of women means the strengthening of their capabilities in the social, political and economic sphere. Women's empowerment and material advancement helps them to improve their economic position. So, if women are to be empowered, it is essential to supply them an increasing network of support services so that they are liberated from some of their gender linked restraints. If women are to be economically empowered, it is fundamental to provide them with additional channels of credit, training, employment, greater exposure, leadership skills and social security. All these necessitate the creation of an environment through suitable policies and programme, institutional arrangements at different levels, and adequate financial resources. Policy makers in India are largely aware of this issue and have launched several innovative schemes for women empowerment not only through Government agencies but also through dedicated non-governmental organizations. Hence the present study is an attempt to analyse empowerment of women on decision making through Self Help Group in Madurai District.

OBJECTIVES OF THE STUDY

The specific objectives of the present study are:

(i) To analyse socio-economic empowerment of women.

(ii) To measure empowerment of women in decision making through self-help group.

(iii) To study the relationship between the level of empowerment and socio economic characteristics of women.

(iv) To identify the factors which influence the empowerment of women.

SAMPLE DESIGN

There are 8,657 women SHGs in the Madurai District with 1,12065 members functioning under Mahalir thittam. Of the total, 7502 are functioning in rural areas and 1153 in urban areas. Proportionate sampling technique was adopted to select 150 sample beneficiaries under SHG—schemes from Mahalir thittam. The primary data were collected through well-structured and comprehensive interview schedule by personal interview method during October 2004 to April 2005.

FRAMEWORK OF ANALYSIS

In order to quantify the economic and social impacts on SHG members, the Economic and Social Empowerment (ESE) Index was computed for each member combining the social and economic parameters using the scoring technique applied by Singh, Padam and Rattan Chand. The parameters and scores assigned to their different level are given in Appendix I & II

The index of social indicators of hth members S_h is given by:

$$\Sigma S_i / \Sigma S_{i(\max)} \qquad \ldots (1)$$

and the index of economic indicators (E_h) is given by

$$\Sigma E_j / \Sigma E_{j(\max)} \qquad \ldots (2)$$

Combined index (ESE model) SLI_h is given by

$$W_1 S_h + W_2 E_h \qquad \ldots (3)$$

Where, S_i and E_j represent *I*th social and *j*th economic indicator, respectively.

$S_{i(\max)}$ and $E_{j(\max)}$ are the maximum scores *i*th social indicator and *j*th economic indicator can take.

Weight W_1 is given by $\Sigma S_i(\max) \Sigma S_i(\max) + \Sigma S_j(\max)$ and W_2 is $(1-W_1)$. The values of $\Sigma S_i(\max)$ and $\Sigma S_j(\max)$ worked out to 7 and 20 respectively. The W_1 and W_2 are 0.26 and 0.74 respectively.

The empowerment of women in the present study has been measured in terms of their decision making capacity which has been classified on the basis of

(a) Self decision
(b) Myself more than husband/family member
(c) Both equal
(d) Husband/family member more than myself and
(e) Husband/family member

These five aspects are applicable for seven variables which are identified for measuring the domestic decision making power of women. The identified variables are:

(i) Preparation of the family budget
(ii) Education of children
(iii) Health and medicine
(iv) Leisure activities
(v) Purchase of home appliances
(vi) Giving away gifts to others and
(vii) Personal needs

The responses have been obtained from the sample women beneficiaries in five aspects for each variable. The responses observed for each variable have been scored. To secure the total empowerment score of a woman beneficiaries, five points are given for "self", four points for "myself" more than husband/ family member, three points are given for "both equal", two points for husband/family member more than myself, one point for "husband/family member" responses. Thus, the total empowerment score of a respondent is obtained by adding up the scores of all seven variables.

LEVEL OF EMPOWERMENT

The level of empowerment has been classified into three categories, namely low level, medium level and high level for analytical purposes. The level of empowerment has been said to be high when the score values are $\geq \overline{x} + SD$ and if the score values are $\leq \overline{x} + SD$ then it has been classified as low level empowerment, while if the score value is between $\overline{x} + SD$ and $\overline{x} - SD$ then it has been classified as medium level empowerment. $\overline{x}$ and *SD* are the arithmetic mean and standard deviation calculated from the score values.

Chi-square Test

In order to examine the relationship between the level of empowerment and socio economic factors, the Chi-square test has been employed.

MULTIPLE LINEAR REGRESSION MODEL

In order to assess the contribution of independent variables to women empowerment, stepwise multiple regression analysis has been carried out.

RESULTS AND DISCUSSION

Economic Empowerment

The economic empowerment is measured with the help of increase in assets value, income, savings, loan amount and family income. The indices of economic indicators of each member are prepared at pre and post-SHG stages. The indices are classified as below 20, 20–40, 40–60, 60–80, 80–100.

The distribution of members according to their economic index at pre and post-SHG stages are presented in Table 1.

It is clearly understood from the above Table 1 that the 32.13 percent of the members have an index below 20 is the pre SHG where as figure declines to 12.64 in the post SHG stage the percentage of members who have an index value of

Table 1. Distribution of Households According to Economic Index

Index	Pre SHG	Post SHG
Below 20	32.13	12.64
20–40	21.60	19.25
40–60	29.45	30.16
60–80	13.48	25.60
Percentage	100	100
Average Value of Index	34.39	53.88

above 80 at the pre SHG is 3.34 and the figure has increased to 12.35 at the post SHG stage.

SOCIAL EMPOWERMENT

The social empowerment of the members of sample SHG member was measured by using the changes in a set of parameters such as improvement in social recognition, participation, self-sufficiency, social communication, social independent, social interaction and social responsibility between pre and post SHG situations. The social index is prepared with the help of seven questions related to the seven social variables which are binary in nature. The social indices of the members are classified as below 20, 20–40, 40–60, 60-80, 80–100. The average value of social index for each group is also calculated. Table 2 presents the details.

The Table 2 reveals that the percentage of members who have the social index value of below 20 has declined from 18.34 in pre SHG to 4.61 in post SHG situations where as the present age for the value of 80 to 100 had increased from 9.02 to 41.95 during the same periods the average value of social index for the members at pre and post SHG situation were 35.47 and 68.66. It indicates that the social empowerment of the members had increased during the two period of study.

Table 2. Distribution of Household According to Social Indices

Index	Pre SHG	Post SHG
Below 20	18.34	4.61
20–40	30.81	5.75
40–60	27.51	18.24
60–80	14.32	29.45
80–100	9.02	41.95
Percentage	100	100
Average Value of Index	35.47	68.66

ECONOMIC AND SOCIAL INDEX IN PRE AND POST SHG SITUATION

The economic and social indices of the members are compared at pre and post SHG stages. The average economic and social indices of the members at two different periods are calculated.

From that the incremental index is drawn. In order to test the significant difference between the two mean values of economic and social index is each sector and also for pooled data the '*t*' statistic is also computed. The resulting average economic index with its '*t*' value is shown in Table 3.

Table 3. Economic and Social Index in Pre and Post SHG Situations

Index	Pre SHG	Post SHG	Incremental Index	'*t*' statistic
Average Economic Index	34.29	52.49	18.20	4.2618*
Average Social Index	39.99	64.25	24.26	2.8907*

* Indicates the Significant at 5% level.

From the above Table 3 for the pooled data the average economic index has increased from 34.29 in pre SHG to 52.49 in post SHG. The average social index has increased from 39.99 in pre SHG situation to 64.25 in post SHG situation. The changes in economic and social index during the two periods and pooled data are statistically significant since its '*t*' values are greater than the respective Table values.

ECONOMIC AND SOCIAL EMPOWERMENT INDEX (ESE)

The ESE index is the combined index of social and economic indices. It is calculated by the product of weight and value of economic and social indices respectively.

The formula applied is $ESE_n = W_1 + S_h + W_2 E_n$ whereas W_1 and W_2 are the weightage and S_h and E_n are the social and economic indices of the members. The weightage W_1 is $\Sigma S_i (max) + S_j (max)]$ and W_2 is $1 - W_1$. The resulting averages of *ESE* index of the members belonging to the both sector and also for the pooled data are shown in Table 4.

Table 4. Average Value of ESE Index Model

Index	Pre SHG	Post SHG	Incremental Index	'*t*' statistic
Average ESE Index	29.49	52.74	23.25	2.0925*

* Indicates the significant at 5% level.

The average ESE index had increasing from 29.49 to 52.74 in pre and post SHG situations. The incremental value in the ESE index is 23.25.

The '*t*' test reveals that the change in ESE index in the pre and post SHG situations are significant.

EMPOWERMENT THROUGH DECISION MAKING

This section attempts to analyse the decision making power enjoyed by women participants/beneficiaries on the variables namely **(i)** Preparation of the family budget, **(ii)** Education of children, **(iii)** Health and medicine, **(iv)** Leisure activities, **(v)** Purchase of home appliances, **(vi)** Giving away gifts for others and **(vii)** personal needs.

The decision making of women beneficiaries on seven variables presented in Table 5.

It has been inferred from the Table that nearly 34.66 percent of the women beneficiaries take independent decision relating to the family budget.

Decision making regarding the education of children here refers to the kind of schools in which they intend to enroll their children, expenses to be made on children, the level of education upto which they want their children to study and so on. It is apparent that, about 38.66 percent (58 respondents) take decisions independently relating to childrens education in their family.

Women have major responsibility to look after the health of their family members. It has been observed that nearly 32.66 percent of the women beneficiaries take independent decisions regarding the health and medicine.

The decision making on the leisure activities, here refers to the recreational activities that is regarding the visit to the cinema theatres, watching televisions, chatting, visiting their relative's houses and so on. Nearly, 40.66 percent of women beneficiaries have been taking decision independently regarding leisure time activities in their family.

Purchases of home appliances are also an important variable for measuring empowerment of women. It is inferred from the Table that 37.33 percent of women beneficiaries were in a position to purchase the home appliances by their own choice.

Table 5. Decision Making on Seven Variables

Final Decision Taken	Preparation of the Family Budget	Education of Children	Health and Medicine	Leisure Activities	Purchase of Home Appliances	Giving away Gifts to Others	Personal Needs%
Self	52 (34.66%)	58 (38.66%)	49 (32.66%)	61 (40.66%)	56 (37.33%)	60 (40%)	64 (42.66%)
Myself more than Husband Family Member	48 (32%)	43 (28.66%)	37 (24.66%)	39 (26%)	42 (28%)	45 (30%)	41 (27.33%)
Both Equal	16 (10.66%)	23 (15.33%)	25 (16.66%)	20 (13.33%)	21 (14%)	22 (14.66%)	21 (14%)
Husband/Family Member more than Myself	12 (8%)	16 (10.66%)	16 (24%)	12.66 (19%)	18 (12%)	17 (11.33%)	15 (10%)
Husband/Family Member	22 (14.66%)	10 (6.6%)	10 (15%)	7.33 (11%)	13 (8.66%)	6 (4%)	9 (6%)
Total	150 (100%)	150 (100%)	150 (100%)	150 (100%)	150 (100%)	150 (100%)	150 (100%)

Source. Survey Data.

Offering of gifts are the means of pleasure in human life. Gifts are given and received during some festivals and on special occasions in our life time. We as members of the society, have to give gifts to others on the occasions such as wedding, birthday and the like. Nearly 40 percent of women beneficiaries have been in a position to take own decision independently regarding the purchase and offering of gifts to others.

The Table exhibits that nearly 42.66 percent of women beneficiaries have been taking their own independent decision regarding their personal needs.

This section attempts to analyse decision making power enjoyed by women beneficiaries on the seven variables with the help of scoring values. It is observed from the total score, that majority of women could take decisions (260–score value) independently relating to family budget. It is understood on the basis of total score (290) value that the women take decision independently on their own with regard to the education of their children. From the Table it is clear that on the basis of total score (245) majority of women beneficiaries could take decisions independently concerned with their family's health and medicine. It could be concluded on the basis of total score value (305) that women beneficiaries have been taking decisions on their own independently regarding the leisure time activities.

It could be concluded that on the basis of total score value (280) women beneficiaries have been taking individual decision regarding purchase of home appliances in the study area. It has been observed on the basis the total. Score value (300) that women have been taking decision on their own independently regarding the gifts to offer others. Finally, it may be observed that the total score value (320) of decisions on the personal needs of women beneficiaries have been taken on their own independently in the study area.

Table 6. Total Scoring on Seven Variables

Final Decision Taken	Preparation of the Family Budget	Education of Children	Health and Medicine	Leisure Activities	Purchase of Home Appliances	Giving Away Gifts to Others	Personal Needs
Self	260	290	245	305	280	300	320
Myself more than Husband Family Member	192	172	148	156	168	180	164
Both Equal	48	69	75	60	63	66	63
Husband/Family Member more then Myself	24	32	48	38	36	34	30
Husband/Family Member	22	10	15	11	13	6	9
Total	546	573	521	570	560	586	586

LEVEL OF EMPOWERMENT

The empowerment of women has been classified into three levels namely low, medium and high on the basis of average score value ($\bar{x}$) and its standard deviation (S.D.). The level of empowerment of women beneficiaries in the study area has been depicted in Table 7.

Table 7. Level of Empowerment of Women Beneficiaries

Level of Empowerment	No. of Women Employees	Percentage
High	88	58.66
Medium	37	24.66
Low	25	16.68
Total	150	100.00

From the Table 7 it is clear that out of 150 sample women respondents 88 (58.66 percentage) fall under high level, 37 (24.66 percentage) come under the category of medium level and 25 (16.68 percentage) fall under low level.

Relationship between the Level of Empowerment and Socio-Economic Factors of Women Beneficiaries

In order to examine the relationship between the level of empowerment and socio-economic factors like age, education, caste, family size, type of family, spouse employment and income of the respondents chi-square test was carried out. The computed results have been summarised in Table 8.

It is inferred from Table 8 that, the calculated chi-square values for age, education, family, size, type of family, spouse's employment and income of the respondents have been found to be greater than the Table value. Thus, it has been significant at

Table 8. The Result of Chi-Square Test between Level of Empowerment and Socio Economic Factors

Final Decision Taken	Calculated Chi-Square Table Value	Degrees Freedom	Chi-Square Value 5% Level	Significance
Age	27.24	4	9.49	Significant
Education	36.27	4	9.49	Significant
Caste	1.72	2	5.99	Not Significant
Family Size	27.36	4	9.49	Significant
Type of Family	18.31	2	5.99	Significant
Spouse Employment	12.13	2	5.99	Significant
Income of Respondent	26.72	4	9.49	Significant

5 percent level. Hence, there exists a relationship between these factors and level of empowerment. As the calculated chi-square value is less than the Table value at 5 percent level in the case of caste, the caste has no influence on the level of empowerment of women in the study area.

ASSESSMENT OF CONTRIBUTION OF INDEPENDENT VARIABLES TO EMPOWERMENT

In order to assess the contribution of independent variables to women empowerment, the step wise multiple regression analysis was carried out. The results are presented in Table 9.

It has been revealed from Table 9 that, three of the variables were entered into the equation and the order of inclusion has been as follows: Income, education and family status. As each of the additional was entered, the multiple R and R^2 increased. This indicates that the income, education, and family status were the best set of predictors of empowerment of respondents having the combined contribution about 97 percent. Allowing one of

Table 9. Summary of Step Wise Multiple Regression

Independent Variable Empowerment

Variables in Equatioon	Multiple R	R^2	F	P	Beta
Income	0.9214	0.79	128.72	0.01	0.92
Education	0.9428	0.81	114.63	0.01	0.36
Family Status (Size)	0.9713	0.83	98.41	0.01	0.08

the independent variables to operate while controlling the other variables in equation, it is clear that it has been the income which had the highest contribution to empowerment of women beneficiaries followed by the education and family status respectively.

MAJOR FINDINGS AND CONCLUSION

The social and economic status of the members have been increased after joining the SHG scheme.

Women beneficiaries have been taking decisions independently on their own regarding the family budget, education of children, family's health and medicine, leisure time activities, purchase of home appliances, offering gifts and personal needs in the study area.

The level of empowerment of women has been classified into three namely high, medium and low levels. The results reveal that majority women beneficiaries fall under high level of empowerment.

The chi-square results reveal that there exists a relationship between the factor *viz.* age, education, family status, type of family, spouse employment and income of the respondents and the level of empowerment where as the caste, have no influence on the level of empowerment of women in the study area.

The step wise multiple regression results reveal that the income has greater contribution to the empowerment of women followed by the education and family status.

CONCLUSION

The participation of women in SHGs has enriched their economic empowerment. The involvement of the women in the group significantly contributes to improvement in the quality of life, social status and confidence of the members. Thus, we can conclude that SHG is one of the significant schemes through which the empowerment of women is achieved.

SUGGESTIONS

The awareness building capacity, skill development and decision making power in home and community should be enhanced in order to widen the scope of women empowerment through SHGs.The Government should take necessary initiatives to bring all women to the mainstream to participate and encourage them to join SHGs and achieve empowerment.

REFERENCES

- Marguerite Berger (1989), "***Giving Women Credit: The Strength and Limitations of Credit as a Tool for Alleviating Poverty***," World Development, Vol. 17, No. 7.
- Sangeetha Purushothaman, ***The Empowerment of Women in India: Grassroots Womens Networks and the States***, Sage Publications, New Delhi, 1998.
- Sushama Sahay (1998), "***Women and Empowerment: Approaches and Strategies***," Discover Publishing House, New Delhi, p. 3.
- Sydney Ruth Schuler and Syed M. Hashemi, "***Defining and Studying Empowerment of Women: A Research Note, from Bangladesh***", J.S.I. Working Paper No. 3, JSI Research and Training Institute, Arlington, V.A., 1993.

APPENDIX- I

Social Index

Social Indicator		
Social Recognition	Others	My Self
Financial Crisis Social by Score	0	?
Social Participation Members of any Society	No.	Yes
Score	0	1
Self Sufficiency are you an Earning Member in	No.	Yes
your Faculty Score	0	1
Social Communication are you	No.	Yes
Communicative in Meeting? Score	0	1
Social Independence are you a Decision Maker	No.	Yes
in your Faculty? Score	0	1
Social Interaction are you an Office Bearer of	No.	Yes
any Society? Score	0	1
Social Responsibility do you React with Social	No.	Yes
Evils? Score	0	1
Social Index		

APPENDIX–II

Economic Index

Economic Indicator					
Asset Value	Nil	<5000	5000–10000	10001–20000	<20000
Score	0	1	2	3	4
Income	<500	500–1000	1001–1500	1501–2000	>2000
Score	0	1	2	3	4
Savings	<100	100–200	201–300	301–400	>400
Score	0	1	2	3	4
Loan Amount	<1000	1000–2000	2001–3000	3001–4000	>4000
Score	0	1	2	3	4
Faculty Income	<1000	1000–2000	2001–3000	3001–4000	>4001
Score	0	1	2	3	4
Economic Index					

Chapter—9

Women Self-Help Groups—A Catalyst for Tribal Development

—Dr. M. Anbalagan*
—V. Selvam**

INTRODUCTION

India has the second largest concentration of tribal population after that of the African continent. About 450 separate tribal groups, speaking more than 100 languages and dialects account for 8.1% of the total population of India. Spread across the country but with concentrations in the North, North-East, Central Tribal Belt and parts of South India. The tribal economy is very poor because the tribal live in underdeveloped areas. Absence of proper transport facilities, communication and socio-economic conditions are the other

* Reader and Head, Post Graduate and Research Department of Commerce Voorhees College, Velore, Tamil Nadu.
** Sr. Lecturer in Management, V.I.T. Business School, Velore Institute of Technology, Vellore, Tamil Nadu.

reasons for the educational weakness. There is enormous human resource potential available in hill areas, which are hither to under utilized or untapped, needs fine tuning for correcting imbalances in the social welfare and social security to the people residing in tribal areas. The present development scenario prevailing in tribal areas tends to emphasize that the tribal people needs protection at all cost from all sorts of exploitation. That warrants the top most priority in order to strengthen the confidence level of a tribal. Once it is built up in the mind set of a tribal, job will be easier for the development administrator to administer the various projects in tribal area.

Need for Study

The world development report of 2005 estimates that 79.9% of India's 1.1 billion population, approximately 175 million families live on less than $2 per day (purchasing power parity) of these approximately 380 million people live in abject poverty, surviving on less than $1 per day. It is now widely acknowledged that micro finance for the poor has enabled numerous families to lift themselves out of poverty. Self Help Movement among the tribal poor, especially women in different parts of the country, is emerging as a very reliable and efficient mode in tribal development and women participation and women empowerment. Apart from financial aspects, it also becomes a platform for exchanging ideas regarding aids prevention, dowry, nutrition, legal marital laws, literacy, sanitation, children rearing etc. During the last decade, India had a tremendous growth of Self-Help Group (SHG) in different forms in different regions. This study makes an effort to contribute something to tribal women SHGs to identify whether there is some relationship between Internal loan given to SHG members and their quality of life.

Review of Literature

1. Shanthudu. D (1993) reviews that the most important cause of tribal discontent appears to be the imbalance in development created by defective planning. Special programmes for the welfare and development of tribal have had only a limited coverage and in practice have become too rigid and uniform in pattern although different approaches and plans are required for solving the problems faced by various tribal groups.
2. Vinod Kumar Mishra (2001) explains that, there is a need to generate self-employment opportunities for tribal disabled people. Instead of selling the raw products to traders at meager rates they can prepare finished or semi finished products and sell them to the government / semi government/ Co-operatives/ trading agencies to fetch better prices.
3. Gurulingaisah. M (2002) discusses the SHGs to meet their felt needs and enable them to participate in planning and implementation of their own development programmmes. Besides, it has been conducting social and health awareness campaigns to eliminate superstitious customs, attitude and thinking related to poverty and child birth which are blocking the progress of tribal women.
4. Vasudevarao (2004) study has shown that the group dynamics through SHGs has brought a change in the attitude and behavior of the tribal, across the Khammam District, Andhra Pradesh.
5. Vipin Sharma (2005) talks about micro finance has demonstrated the potential of building the social capital of the poorest communities.

Objectives of the Study

1. To identify the factors that lead to get internal loan from groups.
2. To find out the quality of life of tribal women SHGs are improved through micro finance.

Hypothesis

Alternative Hypothesis. H1. There is significant level of relationship between internal loan and quality of SHG members life.

METHODOLOGY

Research Design. Research design is descriptive in nature.

Sample Design. The sample consists of tribal women SHGs in Vellore District, Tamil Nadu. The sample size is 150. Convenience sampling method is adopted for selecting samples for the study.

Data Collection

A structured questionnaire was designed to collect data for the study. The questionnaire was divided into two sections. The first section identifies internal loan to members. The second identifies the quality of life of members. The questionnaire consist of both open-ended and close-ended questions.

Analytical Tools

1. Percentage analysis is used to analyze the data collected.
2. Pearson Chi-square test is used to measure the level of significant relationship between internal loan and quality of life of SHGs.

Limitations of the Study

The study is confined to tribal SHGs in Vellore District, Tamil Nadu only. Samples have been selected from tribal women SHGs who got micro finance from banks only.

Analysis and Interpretation

Internal loan to members and quality of SHG members life improved or not.

Table 1.

Quality of Life	Frequency	Percentage
Improved	102	68
Not Improved	48	32
Total	150	100

Source. Primary Data, 2006.

Table 2. Cross Tabulation

Internal	Life		Total
	Improved	Not Improved	
Goat	39	27	66
Agriculture	39	20	59
Self Employed	24	1	25
Total	102	48	150

Source. Primary Data, 2006.

Testing of Hypothesis

Table 3. Chi-Square Test

	Value	df	Asymp. Sig. (2-Sided)
Pearson Chi-square	11.512	2	.0003
Likelihood Ratio	14.800	2	.0001
Linear-by-Linear Association	9.491	1	.0002
No. of Valid Cases	150		

Source. Primary Data, 2006.

Inference

The calculated value of chi-square is .0003. Significant at 5% level (*i.e.*, 1.96). Since the table value is more than the calculated value, We reject the Null Hypothesis (Ho) and accept the Alternative Hypothesis (H1).

Findings

1. Out of 150 respondents 66 respondents are got loan and invested in Goat business, 59 respondents are invested their loan amount in Agricultural activities and 25 respondents are invested their loan amount in self employed activities.
2. Out of 66 respondents only 39 respondents engaged in Goat business indicated that the quality of life is improved and 27 respondents engaged in Goat business indicated that the quality of life is not improved even after getting micro credit from bank.
3. Out of 59 respondents, 39 respondents are engaged in Agricultural activities indicated that the quality of life is improved and only 20 respondents are indicated that the quality of their life is not improved.
4. Out of 25 respondents, 24 respondents are engaged in Self Employed business strongly indicated that the quality of life is improved and only one respondent said the quality of life is not improved.
5. By seeing the overall study, out of 150 respondents 102 respondents (68%) strongly stated that the quality of tribal women SHGs life is improved only after getting internal loan from SHGs through Banks. Only 48 respondents (32%) stated that the quality of tribal women SHGs life is not improved.

CONCLUSION

It is found that the tribal women SHGs in India who got micro credit from banks through groups, have improved their quality of life. Thus the major challenge before the nation today is to evolve appropriate strategy for tribal SHGs to mobilizing the human resource for optimizing use of the available financial resources. Microfinance to tribal SHGs provides a medium for ensuring this by optimizing use of the financial resources. The task force on employment opportunities, while referring to the limitation of the formal financial system in meeting the credit needs of the informal sector, has underlined the importance of micro finance through tribal SHGs as a potentially useful viable channel for generation of employment in the coming year. Not withstanding the fact that the net incremental income to the beneficiaries availing micro credit has been small, the noteworthy feature of micro finance has been the confidence, managerial and entrepreneurial, ability development in the beneficiary, which enables them to take up any other economic activity in a viable manner. This makes the concept of micro finance extremely important for a developing country. Once provision of micro finance is tied up with support given under other schemes for training, acquisition of assets etc., the beneficiary will be able to increase income substantially, which will in turn be of great help in establishing an egalitarian society as envisaged in our Constitution.

REFERENCES

- Gurulingaiah, M. (2002) "***Role of NGO in Empowerment of Tribal Women in Karnataka***," Kurukshetra, A Journal of Rural Development, pp. 30–33.
- Lakshmaiah, T. (2001) "***Tribal Development—Need to Evolve People Oriented Approach***," Kurukshetra, A Journal of Rural Development, Vol. 50. No. 2, pp. 18–21.
- Meenakshi Hooja (2004) "***The Evolving Tribal Development Policies and Startegies in India—A Focus on the Central Tribal Belt***," Sajosps, An International Journal, pp. 8–11.
- Pankaj Naithani (2001) "***Micro Financing the Self Employment Activities***," Kurukshetra, A Journal of Rural Development, Vol. 49, No. 10, pp. 12–14.

- Panda, S. K. (2003) "***Micro Finance in Economic Empowerment of Weaker Sections***," A Development of Journal of Yojana, pp. 21–25.
- Rita Jain, Kushawaha, R.K. Srivastava, A. K. (2003) "***Socio-Economic Impact Through Self Help Groups***," A Development of Journal of Yojana, pp. 11–12.
- Shanthudu, D. (1993) "***Operational Optimization***," Social Welfare, pp. 3–8.
- Vinod Kumar Mishra (2001) "***Employment Opportunities for Tribal Disabled***," A Development of Journal of Yojana, Vol .45, pp. 43–47.
- Vipin Sharma (2005) "***Micro Finance in India—Coming of Age***," Chartered Financial Analyst, Vol. XI, Issue 11, pp. 80–82.

Tribal SHGs Started Goat Business through Micro Finance

Tribal SHGs Marketing their Tamarind in Weekly Market

Awarded Branded Products of Tribal SHGs—Photo from Sem—Tribal, Yelagiri Hills, Tamil Nadu

Tribal SHGs Marketing their Tamarind in Weekly Market

Awarded Branded Products of
Tribal SHGs—Photo from Sem—Tribal, Yelagiri Hills,
Tamil Nadu

Chapter—10

Women Self-Help Groups—A Tool for Women Empowerment in India

—*Dr. R. Karthikeyan**

—*Dr. K. Ramakrishnan***

Women are the noblest of Gods creation supreme in their own sphere of activist.

—**Mahatma Gandhi**

INTRODUCTION

Women are the builders and molders of nation's destiny. Though delicate and soft as lily she has a heart for stronger and bolder than man. She is the supreme inspiration for man's owned march, an embodiment of love, pity and compassion. Women constitute half of the

* Lecturer in Economics, Post Graduate and Research Department of Economics, A.V.C. College (Autonomous), Mannanpandal, Mayiladuthurai, Tamil Nadu.

** Lecturer in Commerce, Post Graduate Research Department of Commerce, A.V.C. College (Autonomous), Mannanpandal, Mayiladuthurai, Tamil Nadu.

human population and their contribution to the socio economic development of a country is vital. Our former president Mr. Fakruddin Ali Ahmed said, "The women of India play a silent, self-effacing role to sustain Indian civilization down the ages." For their greater participation in national life it is necessary that they should occupy position at the decision-making and planning levels. But, the reality is different. In India, poverty in general and extreme poverty in particular has a significant gender dimensions. Women are the most vulnerable group affected by poverty. Rural women play critical role in the process of moving their families out of poverty, around 30% to 35% of the rural Indian households are estimated as headed by women. Even when there is a male earner, women earning forms a significant part of the income of poor households. Thus, increasing role of women is an important strategic necessity for improving the society as a whole.

Women Empowerment is recognized globally as a key element at the Millennium Summit held in New York in 2000. In order to promote the women empowerment and protect their rights, the General Assembly of UN adopted "Convention on the Elimination of all forms of Discrimination against Women" on 18th December 1979 which came into force on 3rd September 1981.

It is recognized that State of women at macro level is very deplorable, because

Two third of world's adult illiterates are women;
Seventy percent of world poor are women;
There is sharp decline in Juvenile sex ratio;
Maternal mortality rate and Infant mortality rate are high;
At all levels there is gender gap in literacy;
Drop out rates is high among girl students;
Incidence of crimes against women is on the increase:
and so on.

However, Fifth Five Year Plan onwards due importance has been given for the empowerment of women in India where the concept of women development was took place in lieu of the concept of women welfare. The Eighth Plan promised to ensure for the provision of importance to women in all sectors of the economy. A special scheme, Rashtriya Mahila Kosh was set up in 1993 to fulfill the credit needs of poor and asset less women. The Ninth Plan made two significant changes in the strategy of planning for women—'empowerment of women' and 'convergence of existing services' available in both women specific and women related sectors. The Tenth Five Year Plan considers 'empowering women as the agent of socio-economic change and development.' Therefore, empowering women folk is need of the hour to maintain socio, economic, political, institutional and psychological development at macro level.

The World Bank defines empowerment as "the process of increasing the capacity of individuals or groups to make choices and to transform those choices into desired actions and outcomes. Central to this process are actions which both build individual and collective assets and improve the efficiency and fairness of the organizational and institutional context which govern the use of these assets. Empowerment is a process of improvement of the quality of life in terms of income, life spans, dignity, decision making in socio economic activities, political participation and psychological autonomy. It is a comprehensive aspects in which the qualitative improvement of life of women is taken place.

The Global Conference on Women's Empowerment, 1988 highlighted empowerment as the surest way of making women 'partners in development'. The Food and Agricultural Organization has also emphasized on strengthening and motivating women at the grassroots. These can be achieved by infusing them with a strong, positive self-image, critical thinking, group cohesion, decision-making and equal participation.

SPHERES OF WOMEN EMPOWERMENT

There are basically four spheres of women empowerment *viz.*, Economic Empowerment, Social Empowerment, Psychological Empowerment and Political Empowerment.

The economic empowerment relates to the process of improving the quality of life in the economic aspects both monetary and value terms. In India, females head about 10 percent of the total households and the ownership of land and other properties are mainly in the name of the male members of the family. Hence, women are hardly able to have any ownership of resources and autonomy to take decision. The occupational distribution of women indicates the gender segregation of tasks and the underlying reality of high illiteracy among female workers, which consigns them to low-paid, unskilled jobs compared to males and they are subject to economic exploitations. This can be possible by measures on the wage payment, provision of women employment, opportunities for increasing earnings, promotion of women entrepreneurship, provisions of asset holdings etc. Thus, female work participation rate is a necessary condition but it is not a sufficient condition for economic empowerment of women and it is possible only when women have full autonomy to spend their income and also control resources.

The social empowerment refers to the process of improving the quality of life of women in social aspects. It is process of reduction of gender discriminations in the name of superstitious beliefs, social functions, religious beliefs, customs, culture, etc. Indian women get less priority in education and are deprived of proper food and lack access to health care. The social empowerment of women is a long and difficult process, as it requires a change in the mind set of the people and this can be possible only by creating awareness among the public and taking severe legal measures against the social discriminations.

The political empowerment refers to the process of improving the quality of women in terms of political participation. Though the political participation of women has been gradually increasing, still the desired level is not reached. This can be possible by encouraging the importance of women education, enunciation of legal steps like reservation policy on power, asset holding, etc.

The psychological empowerment is the process of improvement in the quality of life of women in terms of their personal and psychological considerations. This can be possible only by creating motivation and developing self-confidence among women through provisions of orientations and opportunities in decision making.

POLICY MEASURES

Empowerment of women is seen as the only means of poverty eradication. So, any economic strategy of empowering women must make provision to link the nature of employment with the skill training required for efficiently running it. Other points needed for improving the same are increased access to credit, marketing, training, skill management, improved technology, enterprise management and social status and power.

There have been a number of measures taken by the Government to ensure for women empowerment at macro level in a sustained manner. The Tenth Plan advocated a three-fold strategy for women empowerment.

Social Empowerment. To create an enabling environment through various affirmative developmental policies and programmes for development of women besides providing them easy and equal access to all the basic minimum services so as to enable them to realize their full potentials.

Economic Empowerment. To ensure provision of training, employment and income generation activities with both forward and backward linkages with the ultimate objectives of making all potential women economically independent and self-reliant; and

Gender Justice. To eliminate all forms of gender discrimination and thus, allow women to enjoy not only the *de jure* but also *de facto* rights and fundamental freedom at par in all sphere *viz.*, political, economic, social, civil. cultural, etc.

THE NATIONAL POLICY FOR EMPOWERMENT OF WOMEN

The National Policy for Empowerment of Women was evolved in the year 2001. It recognizes the causes of gender inequality which are related to social and economic structure. The policy underlines the need for mainstreaming gender perspective in the development process.

OBJECTIVES

Creation of an environment for positive social and economic policies for the development of women to enable them to realize their potential.

The *de jure* and *De facto* enjoyment of all human rights by women on equal basis with men in all spheres—political, economic, social, cultural and civil.

Equal access to participation and decision-making in social, political and economic life of the nation.

Equal access to health care, quality education at all levels, Carrier and vocational guidance, employment and equal remuneration.

Strengthening of legal systems aimed at elimination of all forms of discrimination against women.

Changing societal attitudes and community practices by active participation and involvement of both men and women.

Mainstreaming the gender perspective in the development process.

Elimination of discrimination and all forms of violence against women and girl child; and

Building and strengthening partnerships with civil society, particularly women's organizations.

A National Perspective Plan for Women (1988–2000) was drafted advocating a holistic approach for the development of women which consist of The National Nutrition Policy, The National Policy on Education; and The National Population Policy.

In addition to that the Government has taken some of the important measures for women empowerment in India, such as

Formulation of National Policy on Women Empowerment—2001;
Observation and Celebration of Women's Day on March 8th;
The Year 2001 was observed as Women Empowerment Year by UN.;
The National Plan of Action for Women, 1976;
Setting up of Commission for Women Rights in 1997;
Creation of National Resource Centre for Women;
Enactment of Dowry Abolition Act;
Eve Teasing Act;
Policy on Reservation for Women. (The Bill was passed in the Parliament);
Formation of Self-Help Groups (SHGs);
Provision of Condensed Courses of Education and Vocational Training (CCEVT);
Provision of Socio-Economic Programmes (SEP) etc.

Thus, empowerment is a multi-dimensional concept and refers to the expansion of freedom of choice and action in all spheres to shape one's life. It also implies control over resources and decisions. For women such freedom is often severely restricted due to various socio economic reasons not only in the household but also in society. However, women's empowerment is a major concern and prime priority activity of all the Self Help Groups, Neighbour Hood Groups, Community Development Societies and Micro Enterprises which enhance the confidence and capabilities and economic status of women folk. In India, women empowerment is still complicated due to gender discrimination, low level of education, low work participation, lack of nutritional status, violence against women, poor health, lack of access to health care and poverty. Hence, the empowerment of women requires a set of asset and capabilities at the individuals and at collective level.

Thus, increasing role of women is an important strategic necessity for improving the welfare of the estimated 60 million Indian households which are still below the poverty line. The most feasible option to generate their own income is through self-employment despite the problems they face in gaining access to assets and resources. The Self-Help Group (SHG) is a viable alternative to achieve the objectives of rural development and to get community participation in all rural development programmes which is organized to disburse micro credit to the rural women for the purpose of making them enterprising women and encouraging them to enter into entrepreneurial activities.

Self-Help Group (SHG) is defined as a set of persons with common interest and having interpersonal relations who agree to share risks and benefits through self-designed rules and reciprocity in behavior. This implies that Self-Help Group can be a formal or informal co-operatives, a self evolved group or non-government organisation promoted group.

The SHGs provide the benefits of economies of scale, cost effective alternative for different financial services, collective learning, democratic and participatory culture, a firm based platform for dialogue and co-operation. Moreover, the benefits of SHGs are based on co-operation rather than competition. It follows the real principle of 'Contribute according to your ability and extract according to your need.' Realising the significance of SHGs in micro credit delivery mechanism, the micro credit funding institutions have established SHGs for the purpose of lending and getting repayment in time. At present in India, there are more than 24,000 SHGs comprising more than 11,10,000 members. Realising the importance of SHGs the Tamil Nadu Open University has introduced a Certificate Course in empowering women through Self-Help Groups.

There have been a few attempts both micro level and macro level made to study the performance of SHGs, ***NABARD*** (1989) ***Gupta** et al.* (1989), ***Shah*** (1993), ***Rao*** (1994), ***Kanitkar*** (1994), ***Misra*** and ***Mali*** (1995), ***Manimekali*** and ***Rajeswari*** (2000), ***T. R. Gurumurthy*** (2000), ***R. K. Ojha*** (2001), to mention a few. So far, comprehensive, studies are little in this aspect and hence an attempt has been made to study SHGs at micro level in a District. The present attempt mainly aims to study the group-wise socio-economic status of members; the social and political participation of the members; and to know whether the SHGs change the socio-economic status its members or not.

To fulfill these objectives, five revenue villages from a rural oriented District of Tamil Nadu, Nagapattinam have been chosen as study area and than SHG from each village *viz.*, Om Sakthi SHG, Deepam SHG, Annai Indra SHG, Annai Teresa SHG, and Gomatha SHG have been selected. Then 60 sample respondents/members of SHGs (12 members from each SHG) have been randomly selected. To analyse the problem, relevant information have been collected through a structured and pre-tested interview schedule from them. The information have been analysed and interpreted by using Arithmetic Mean, Standard Deviation, Co-efficient of variation and Student '*t*' Distribution.

SOCIAL PROFILE OF THE MEMBERS

It is found from the study that 66% of the members are SC respondents, 31% are most backward community and only 3% are backward community respondents. No one from the forward community became the members of SHG. With regard to the educational status maximum members *i.e.*, about 55% are primary educated and 45% members are illiterate. Among the total sample respondents, 86% are landless labourers and rest of the 14% are equally distributed to marginal farmers and small farmers. It is also found that more than two-third (72%) of the members live in thatched house and rest of the 28% live in small titled houses.

ECONOMIC PROFILE OF THE MEMBERS

The sources of income of the respondents are identified as farm income; income from farm labour; livestock and poultry; and small business and trade. It is found from the study that the maximum amount of income from farm is calculated to Rs.13500 and the minimum income is calculated Rs. 4300. However, out of 9 farmers 6 earn Rs.11000 & above and 3 members earn below Rs. 5500. It is also found that all the members are going for agricultural occupation. However, 43% of members earn from their labouring out above Rs. 2500 and only 13% members earn less than Rs.1000 in this category. Out of the respondents, 63% posses cattle and poultry, of them 45% members earn below Rs. 1000 from their livestock and the rest of them earn more than Rs. 2000 per annum from the source. Further, 33% members have owned their own small business and trade such as petty shop, tea stall etc., Of them, 70% earn from Rs. 2000 to Rs. 2500 and remaining, 30% earn less than Rs. 2000.

Similarly, the total expenditure constitute the expenditure on food items and expenditure on non-food items. In the present study, the maximum of 41% of the members have spent below

Rs. 500 per month on food items and only 13% members have spent more than Rs. 1500 per month. Similarly in the case of expenditure on non-food items one-third of the total members have spent from Rs. 500 to Rs.1000 and only 24% members have spent above Rs.1500, of them 80% belong to Annai Teresa SHG. However, no members from Annai Indira and Gomatha SHGs have spent more than Rs.1500.

With regard to the borrowing details, in addition to the purpose of the formation of SHGs, 48% members have borrowed. Of them 34% have borrowed from Rs. 2001 to Rs. 3000 and only 4 members who belong to Deepam SHG, as the maximum debt of, more than Rs. 4800. It is a striking finding that no member from Annai Teresa borrowed any amount. Similarly 36% of the respondents have saved, of them 24% have saved below Rs. 3000 (minimum) and 8 members (each 4 from Annai Indra and Gomatha Group) have saved more than Rs.5000 and rest of 64% respondents have not saved any amount.

It is found from the analysis that 65% of the members have interested in political participation and remaining 35% are not. Further, nearly 78% of the members have happily echoed that the SHGs have improved their social status and 85% of respondents have happily opined that their economic status has been improved. From this it could be very obvious to observe that the SHGs are the promising organization for women empowerment. With regard to the observation on the functioning of SHGs, more than 69% have fully satisfied with the functions of their respective SHGs and only one respondent who belongs to Annai Teresa group has satisfied with the functioning of the group.

To know the impact of SHGs on the economic status of its members *i.e.*, whether the Self-Help Groups promote the economic status of its members, the income and expenditure have been compared. To measure the extent of differences the students "*t*" test has been used and it is found that there is one percent level of significant difference registered in the economic status of its members *i.e.*, both the income and expenditure of the members of all SHGs have been fabulously increased after the formation of SHG invariably.

To conclude, the SHGs made a silent revolution in the rural women folk by enabling them to become self-dependant and self-reliant; providing a forum for members for discussing their socio-economic problems; developing decision-making capacity and leadership qualities among members; and equipping women with basic skills required for understating monetary transaction. It can be rightly observed that the SHGs ensure for linking by a common bond like caste, sub-caste, community, place of origin or activity. These groups are also called "Solidarity Group" as they provide monetary and also moral support to individual members in times of difficulty. In a nutshell, the SHGs ensure for women empowerment in all dimensions such as economic empowerment, social empowerment, political empowerment and of course in psychological empowerment.

REFERENCES

- Arundhati Chattopadhyay (2005), "***Women and Entrepreneurship***", YOJANA, Vol. 49, January.
- Bhagyalakhmi. J (2004), "***Women's Empowerment: Miles to Go***", YOJANA, Vol. 48, August.
- Dinkar Rao (1994), "***Self-Help Group and Credit***" Artha Vijnana, Vol. XXXVI, No. 3, September, pp. 194–208.
- Gurumoorthy T. R. (2000), "***Self-Help Groups Empower Rural Women***", Asian Journal of Economic and Social Studies, p. 11.
- Karthikeyan R. (2006), "***Women Self-Help Group in Tamil Nadu—A Micro Level Analysis***", MAYUR,—AVC College Publication, Mayiladuthurai.
- Lakshmi S. and R. Karthikeyan (2000), ***"Changing Role of Women in Economic Development of India" in Development***

that Lasts (ed), New Age International Publishers Pvt. Ltd. New Delhi.

- Manimekalai N. and G. Rajeswari (2000), "***Empowerment of Women through Self-Helf Groups—SHGs***" Margin, Vol. 32, No. 4, July–September, pp. 74–85.
- Manoharan Nair K. and B. Girija (2005), "***Micro Credit—The New Development Paradigm for Poverty Eradication and Women Empowerment***", YOJANA, Vol. 49, January.
- Miller, Dyncan (1998), "***Self-Help and Popular Participation in Rural Water System***" Oxford and IBH, Pvt. Ltd. New Delhi.
- Ojha R. K. (2001), "***Self-Help Groups and Rural Employment***" Yojana, Vol. 45, May, pp. 20–23.
- Sathya Sundaram, I. (1999), "***Rural Development***" B. R. Publishing Corporation, New Delhi.
- Sakuntala Narasimman (1998), "***A Silent Revolution***" The Hindu, May 24.
- Sukgpal Singh (1995), "***Self-Help—Groups in Indian Agribusiness; Reflection from Case Studies***". Artha Vijana, Vol. XXXVI, No. 4, December, pp. 380–388.

Chapter—11

Self-Help Groups—The Panacea for Empowerment of Women

—*K. Kalaichelvi**

INTRODUCTION

In a vast country like India that is marked by the prevalence of innumerous socio-economic and political problems concerted effort is needed to overcome various factors that impeding economic growth. In this growth process Government alone cannot eliminate those problems but the involvement of all citizens without gender bias is warranted. Since women continue to be one half of the segment of population in India, we could not afford to keep them out of the mainstream. They are vital and productive towards India's national economy. But there is a significant gap between their potential and actual productivity. The shift from subsistence to a market economy due to globalisation also has dramatic negative impact on women. In this

* Lecturer in Commerce, Post Graduate and Research Department of Commerce, St. Joseph College (Autononous) Trichy, Tamil Nadu.

regard it is apt to recall the words of UN Secretary General Kofi Annan who emphasized that, gender equality Is more than a goal in itself, it is a precondition for meeting the challenge of reducing poverty, promoting sustainable development and building good governance.[1]

The plight of women in India compared to the global scenario could be visualized from the report published by World Bank recently. It points out that the female literacy in India is 58 percent whereas this figure is 70.4 in the developing world and 77.6 in the world. The school enrolment figures also reveal the poor condition of women in India. It records 47 percent in the case of India. These figures are 57 and 62 percents in developing countries and world respectively.[2] Hence transforming the prevailing social discrimination against women should be given the top priority and must happen concurrently with increased direct action to improve rapidly the social and economic status of women.

Of late, our perspective in the development of women has undergone a radical change. We have moved essentially from a welfare approach where the focus was on the role of women as mothers and wives to an empowerment and rights based approach, where we acknowledge that women have rights which have to be recognized to allow for her full development.

NEED FOR WOMEN'S EMPOWERMENT

Today, it is urgently felt that women should be empowered socially and economically to become a strong and vigorous force in the development of the country.

So in terms of policies and programmes, we have to move from the concept of women's development to women's

---

[1] Carol and Coonrod, "***Chronic Hunger and the Status of Women in India,***" June 1990.

[2] *Ibid.* Carol and Coonrod.

participation in the social, economic and political affairs and then finally to women's empowerment.

Empowerment is a multifaceted process, which encompass many aspects enhancing awareness, increasing access to resource economic, social and political. But of which an equally important component is the mobilization and organization of women into groups, because these groups form the basis for solidarity, strength and collective action.

Empowerment is defined as the processes by which women take control and ownership of their lives through expansion of their choices. Thus, it is the process of acquiring the ability to make strategic life choices in a context where this ability has previously been denied. The core elements of empowerment have been defined as agency (the ability to define one's goals and act upon them), awareness of gendered power structures, self-esteem and self-confidence.[3]

The idea of empowerment is based on active participation by deciding to accept responsibility and thereby gaining power over one's life. This may lead to the emergence of a sense of strength which allows the process to exert control and build up her self-confidence giving opportunities to take part in community life become viable possibilities. India being a democratic country with welfare orientation has recognized that the best way to enable the country to improve in all aspects is through gender equality, women empowerment which must take the form of social mobilization of women into self-help groups.

There are good reasons to target women. The World Bank reports that societies that discriminate on the basis of gender have greater poverty, slower economic growth, weaker governance and a lower standard of living.

---

[3] Kabeer, N., "***Resources, Agency, Achievements Reflections on the Measurement of Women's Empowerment***," 2001, SIDA Studies No. 3.

INGREDIENTS OF EMPOWERMENT OF WOMEN

The empowerment of women must be emphasized at three levels. They are social and economic empowerments and capacity building in some specified aspects.

The social empowerment includes **(1)** equal status, participation and power of decision making of the women at household, community and village level **(2)** overcoming social, cultural and religious barriers to achieve equality in status and recognition of women in their day to day affairs and matters concerning them and, **(3)** participation and power of decision making in democratic institutions.

The economic empowerment includes **(1)** creation of accessibility to financial resources outside the households **(2)** reducing vulnerability of the poor women to critical situations like famine, flood, tsunami and other risks **(3)** significantly increasing women's own income and power to retaining such income and thereby making their own decision to spend it **(4)** enhancing their accountability to allocate the household and other incomes for the purposes decided by them.

Capacity building regarding better awareness on health education, environment, legal rights etc., improving functional literacy, communication skill, leadership skill, self help and mutual helps.

Empowerment in these three levels would lead to overall improvement of women individually and as group member by providing adequate income generating activities through wage and self employment. Through ripple-effect this would benefit the other poor families in the community and village as a whole in the long run.

Along with these three levels two vital processes have been identified as important for empowerment. The first is social mobilization and collective agency, as poor women often lack the basic capabilities and self-confidence to counter and challenge existing disparities and barriers against them. Often, change agents are needed to catalyse social mobilization consciously, second, the process of social mobilization needs to be accompanied and complemented by economic security.

With the above brief conceptual understanding of empowerment, what strategies can be used effectively to empower women? In many developing countries, one strategy which has been found to be promising is the formation of self-help groups, with effective participation of women members often coupled with savings and microcredit loans.

In order to bring women to the centre-stage of development and thereby ensuring better participation in the developmental efforts of our nation, self help groups are instrumental in assimilation and dissemination of knowledge of the requirements for social and economic empowerment.

EMPOWERMENT THROUGH SELF HELP GROUPS

Whatever ingredients required for the empowerment of women are developed and promoted through self help groups. The women members of self help groups are exposed to the features like (1) common experience of the members (2) mutual help and support, (3) the helper principle, *i.e.,* those who helps others with a common problem get benefited the most from the exchange, (4) differential association that emphasizes the reinforcement of self concepts of normality which hastens the individuals separation from commitment to their previous deviant identities (5) collective will power and belief that is the tendency of each person to look at others in the group for validation of her feelings and attitudes (6) importance of information. The promotion of greater factual understanding of the problem, condition as opposed to intra psychic understanding (7) constructive action towards shared goals. This is based on the notion that the groups are action-oriented and their philosophy is that members learn by doing and are changed by doing.

The involvement of women in self help groups thus has made them discover their inner strength, gain self-confidence, and women in rural areas find a new identity.

EMPOWERMENT THROUGH SELF HELP MICRO CREDIT SCHEMES

The SHG-Bank linkage programme started by NABARD in 1992 has emerged as the major micro finance programme in the country. About 90 percent of the groups linked with banks were exclusively women groups.

The linkage between self help groups and banks makes women to be self reliant in financial matter. It helps in overcoming the problems of high transaction costs in providing credit to the poor. The SHGs also offer ways of overcoming the problem of collateral physical access and excessive documentation which reduced the capacity of formal institution to serve the women and thereby poor families.

Self-help groups intermediated by microcredit have been shown to have positive effects on women, with some of these impacts being ripple effects. They have played valuable roles in reducing the vulnerability of the poor, through asset creation, income and consumption smoothing, provision of emergency assistance, and empowering and emboldening women by giving them control over assets and increased self-esteem and knowledge.[4] Several recent assessment studies have also generally reported positive impacts.[5]

---

[4] Zaman. H., and "Assessing the Poverty and Vulnerability Impact of Micro Credit in Bangladesh: A case study of BRAC," 2001.

[5] Simanowitz et al., "Ensuring Impact: Reaching the Poorest while Building Financially Self Sufficient Institutions, and Showing Improvement in their Lives of the Poorest Women and their Families," 2002.

From field visits and from various documented sources, it would appear that financial services, especially microcredit, provided to self-help groups have brought about an increase in household income. In India, studies in microcredit done on groups dealing with dairy farming have noted positive profit levels and short payback periods for loans.[6] Earnings generated from such undertakings have been instrumental in increasing the physical well-being of the household, often through better nutrition and sanitation. The household's asset base has also been enhanced by the addition of jewellery (a portable asset), improved housing and land purchase in some cases.

The growth and achievement of self help groups in recent years in India show an advancement in the life style of women towards empowerment. The growth of self help groups enhanced their participation in national development and decision making process. Following Tables analyse the growth of self help groups, their achievement in town panchayats of various districts of Tamil Nadu and financial assistance received by these SHGs.

Table 1. Growth Rate of Self Help Groups in India

Year	No. of SHGs	Growth of SHGs	%
1999–00	81780	48785	
2000–01	149050	67370	82
2001–02	197653	48603	32
2002–03	255882	58229	29
2003–04	361731	105849	41
2004–05	539365	177634	49

Source. Economic Survey, 2006.

6 Lalitha. N., and Nagarajan B. S., "Self Help Groups in Rural Development," 2002.

Table 2. Achievement of SHGs in the Town Panchayats of Various Districts in Tamil Nadu

Districts	No. on New Groups to be Formed	No. of Groups Formed	Achievement (%)
Kancheepuram	600	1297	216
Thiruvallur	325	804	247
Vellore	550	384	70
Thiruvannamalai	250	260	104
Darmapuri	250	341	136
Krishnagiri	175	174	99
Salem	825	889	108
Namakkal	475	585	123
Erode	1325	2032	153
Coimbatore	1300	1599	123
Nilgiris	275	536	195
Cadalore	400	605	151
Villupuram	375	704	188
Tanjore	550	966	176
Nagapattinam	200	522	261
Thiruvarur	175	409	234
Tiruchirapalli	425	418	98
Perambalur	150	180	120
Pudukottai	200	175	88
Dindugal	600	1318	220
Karur	275	364	132
Madurai	300	172	57
Theni	550	316	57
Ramanathapuram	175	92	53
Virudhunagar	225	257	114
Sivaganga	300	136	45
Tirunelveli	900	1340	149
Tuticorin	475	1230	259
Kanyakumari	1400	3349	239
Total	14025	21454	153

Source. Directorate of Town Panchayat D:/SHG.Htm.

The growth rate of self help groups in India highlights a positive trend from 2000–01 to 2004–05. The initiative taken by the Government and NGOs has paved the way for its constant growth.

The SHGs formed in town panchayats have performed well in achieving their goals.

The Table 2, very clearly points out the achievement of self help groups formulated in the town panchayats of various Districts of Tamil Nadu. The special features of these self help groups are that the members belong to BPL families and 80 percent of them are women folks.

The achievement of SHGs in all the Districts is remarkable. Seven Districts have crossed 200 percent achievements and 13 Districts have crossed 100 percent level. All these achievements finally tell upon the empowerment of women folks in all the districts of Tamil Nadu.

Table 3. Outreach of SHGs and Bank Linkage in India

Aspects	2000	2001	2002
% of Women's Group	85	90	90
Average of Loan per SHG	16814	18227 (8.4%)	22240 (22%)
Average Loan per Family	1016	1072 (5.5%)	1316(22.8%)

Source. NABARD and Micro finance 2001–2002.

The significant achievement made by SHGs could be observed by its linkage with banks for its financial support. The Table 3 shows the growth of average loan extended to its members and their families.

The average loan extended per SHG increased by 22 percent in 2002. The average loan extended per family also increased by 22.8 percent in 2002.

STEPS TO BE TAKEN TO STRENGTHEN SHGs

The rural and urban divide in India has to be taken into account before the formation and operation of SHGs. In rural areas the women folk need an initiation which is entirely different from that of urban areas.

In fact, requirements for empowerment of rural women are to be identified based on their role and the degree of gender inequality in their society.

The Government and other organizations while forming SHGs in rural and urban societies have to consider the social and economic background of the women in those respective societies. Then only the means for women empowerment could be set properly.

A number of schemes such as Swayamsiddha, Swablamban and Support to Training cum Employment Programme (STEP) are in progress which pave the way for viable SHGs in getting trained in various income generating activities. (Economic Survey, page–218).

Rashtriya Mahila Kosh is helpful in getting in various traditional trades and crafts (such as poultry, bee keeping and weaving) as well as newly emerging vocations (such as IT sector) or skill upgradation and capacity building.

CRITICAL APPRAISAL OF SELF HELP GROUPS

In traditional societies, women's empowerment does not occur easily or overnight. It was most noticeable among certain types of women. Perhaps one of the most important emerging lessons is that women's groups themselves in their social aspects, play a role in such empowerment. This argues for placing emphasis on sustaining groups beyond the life of the project, which indeed was done in this instance. The project evaluation also recommended that communication support (films, radio, broadcasts and so on, with sensitization and training content) is to be used to speed up the empowerment process.

Four of the main processes that could lead to women's empowerment as defined by the International Fund for Agricultural Development (IFAD)[7] evaluation were-as follows.

Changes in Women Mobility and Interaction

The evaluation found that women had become more mobile and begun to have new interaction with a range of officials. There was even a growing willingness on the part of group members to approach the government officials.

Changes in Women's Labour Patterns

The evaluation did not find any major changes in gender division of labour. There was comparatively greater change reported in non-domestic productive tasks. Not all the changes in such labour patterns were mixed and not as positive as along other dimensions.

Changes in Women's Access to and Control over Resources

It seems that a number of the groups undertook activities that would give their communities better infrastructural or services. In their sense they played a key role in promoting changes in collective access to resources.

Changes in Intra-Household Decision-Making

There seemed to be a slight improvement in women's involvement in household decision-making in male-headed

[7] D:/Women% 20 Empowerment.htm.

households. However, the traditional gender-based division persist in intra-household decision making. But group members had become more aware of the property and political rights. As in the case of mobility and social interaction, the evaluation again found greater improvements among women heads of households, older women and more educated women.

Studies in several countries point out that loans are sometimes used for consumption smoothing, not production. It has been-pointed out that the poor often have short-term liquidity needs (frequently requiring lump-sum payments), which would normally be met by usurious moneylenders if other financial sources such as micro credit were not available. Sudden and debilitating shocks can force poor households into disempowering situations of distress.[8]

Self-help groups, especially linked to micro credit schemes, have not been without their critics, nor are they a panacea for meeting challenges in economic and social development. It is widely recognized that such schemes are not universally successful. For example, some studies have shown that micro credit will not work in locations that do not have sufficient cash-based market activity, are isolated and with low population densities, or are largely self-contained with few outside ties.

Some critics have pointed out that while micro credit schemes can reduce, vulnerability, they have not lifted women out of abject poverty or have taken a long time to demonstrate any significant impact. On their own, micro credit schemes have limitations as they cannot transform social relations and the structural causes of poverty.

Critics have charged that micro credit accessed by women has often been appropriated or hijacked by other household

8 Social Safety Nets for Women, ESCAP, 2002.

members, leaving women burdened with the responsibility of repayment and the sanctions of default.

Certain field reports suggest that, there are certain SHGs which are contrary to the vision for development, they are generally not composed of mainly the poorest families. There is greater evidence of social empowerment of women members rather than significant and consistent economic impact and the financial skills of group members have not developed as planned.

CONCLUSION

The multiple aspects of self-help groups developed in a phased process, starting with economic enhancement, leading to empowerment at the individual level, and then moving on to collective action at the community level. It also shows that various Government bodies can play supportive roles. However, these initiatives will not be able to bring about social transformation in the aggregate unless issues of control and ownership of the production process, linkages with a broader market and greater decision-making at the political level are tackled. Initiatives at the community level can be a useful tool to empower women, forging gender equality from the grass-roots to the national level. However, these initiatives have to incorporate strategies and measures that empower the poor, especially poor women, and enable them to participate in the development and transformation of society.

REFERENCES

- Carol and Coonrod, "***Chronic Hunger and the Status of Women in India***," June 1990.
- Ibid. Carol and Coonrod.
- Kabeer, N., "***Resources, Agency, Ahievements Reflections on the Measurement of Women's Empowerment***," 2001, SIDA Studies No. 3.

- Zaman. H., and ***"Assessing the Poverty and Vulnerability Impact of Micro Credit in Bangladesh: A Case Study of BUAC,"*** 2001.
- Simanowitz *et al.*, ***"Ensuring Impact : Reaching the Poorest while Building Financially Self-Sufficient Institutions, and Showing Improvement in their Lives of the Poorest Women and their Families***:, 2002.
- Lalitha, N., and Nagarajan B.S., ***"Self-Help Groups in Rural Development,"*** 2002.
- D:/Women% 20 Empowerment.htm.
- Social Safety Nets for Women, ESCAP 2002.

Chapter—12

Grassroots Women Entrepreneurship through Self-Help Groups

—N. Mukundan*
—B. Sumathi**

INTRODUCTION

In recent years women are making their mark even in the field of business activities. Such a mark shows greater attention to promote self employment among women population. Special training programmers are organized for women to enable them to start their own ventures. Financial Institutions and Nationalized Banks have also set up special cells to assist women entrepreneurs. But the efforts to develop entrepreneurship among women are focused more on urban

* Lecturer in Economics, Post Graduate and Research Department of Economics, A.V.C. College (Autonomous), Mannampandal, Mayiladuthurai, Tamil Nadu.

** M.Phil. Research Scholar, Post Graduate and Research Department of Economics, A.V.C. College (Autonomous), Mannampandal, Mayiladuthurai, Tamil Nadu.

women. The problems faced by women in rural areas are more serious and different in many respects than the problems faced by the women in urban areas. Urban women have access to better education, better facilities and a varieties of opportunities when compared to rural women. Rural women lack of motivation, to undertake any non-traditional economic activity. In addition to this the rural traditional women are still subjected to discriminate treatment from childhood. Hence, rural women are incapacitated to pursue any independent economic activity. In this context, emergence of rural women entrepreneurship in rural economy is an indicator of women's independence and their improved social status in rural areas. Hence, the present study makes an attempt to highlight those problems as well as to suggest suitable remedial measures for women entrepreneurship at grassroots level.

WOMEN ENTREPRENEURS IN INDIA

The emergence of women entrepreneurs in a society depends to a great extent on the economic, social, psychological and other factors. As far as India is concerned, the presence of entrepreneurs is vital necessity to achieve rapid all around development of the country. It also helps in tapping the inherent talent prevailing among them and acts as a panaceas for many problem faced by them such as dowry, low recognition in society, poverty, unemployment and excessive dependence on male members. With the spread of education and the awareness of women entrepreneurs are shifted from the extended kitchen activities and traditional cottage industries to the higher levels of activities, *i.e.*, a shift from 3Ps., (Powder making, Pickle making and Pappad making) to 3 Es., *viz.* (Engineering, Electronics and Energy). It can be noted that women are putting up units to manufacture solar-cookers (Gujarat), T.V. Capacitors (Orissa) and electronic ancillaries (Kerala). The 150 women entrepreneurs from all over Maharashtra and 75 women from Pune city have reported that are running the following types of industries of their own namely engineering, electronics fabrics, eatables, ready made garments, poultry, handicrafts, nursery, toy making, cup making, plastic goods, drugs, paintings and miscellaneous. Thus, women entrepreneurs are rapidly coming up not only in the field of tiny and small-scale entrepreneurship but also shifting gradually to modern technology fields.

GRASSROOT WOMEN ENTREPRENEURSHIP THROUGH SHGs

Information and communication technologies make the role of time and distance less significant in organizing business and production related activities. As a result of the technology a high proportion of jobs outsourced by firms are going to women; therefore they can work any where, and any time and raise their income to become more financially independent and empowered. At the grassroots, presently many development agencies are planning their programmes and projects of the empowerment of women through capacity building and strengthen their organizations. Given the importance of female leadership in community and grassroot level organizations, non-governmental organization have been identified as a key actor in empowering women and in ensuring them an accurate knowledge of their true situation, of their actual and potential roles and obstacles to their economic participation. Training in production skills is combined with access to markets and credit based on the need to deal with conflicting interests of the rich and the poor in a community. In the villages, poor women have been gradually gaining confidence and learning how to handle complex business through SHGs.

NEED FOR THE STUDY

The precipitation of women entrepreneurs in the economic activities is now emerging as a universal phenomenon. The advent of information age has infused new confidence in the minds of women entrepreneurs. The information technology and service sector, has given more opportunities to the women entrepreneurs. In addition to this technological improvement in every sphere of economic activity simplifies the process and procedures which in turn helps the women to make easy entry into many businesses. Hence, the present day women, being educated do not matter at all to undertake any venture. As the cost of living increases day-by-day all the members of the family are to earn something which also compels the women to redefine the roles at home and outside. Above all, the women entrepreneurs must be encouraged to their economic potentialities. The women becoming self employed is the only way of solving the unemployment problems prevailing among the women.

RESEARCH PROBLEM

Rural women's self employment in the informal sector is based on various types of activities *viz.*, farm-based activities and allied activities, home based production, retail trading and services like vegetable selling, garment making, catering, petty shop etc.. The perpetuating State of high interest payment, low income, insecurity of work opportunities, clutches of the private money lenders and the vicious circle of indebtedness, all such factors push up to the 'feminization of poverty'. However, there are ample studies in metropolitan and other capital cities wherein women are engaged in some kind of entrepreneurial activities. But, studies on women entrepreneurship at grassroots level through SHGs are very limited. For this purpose the present research study attempts to examine the women entrepreneurship at grassroots with reference in Mappadugai village, Mayiladuthurai Taluk, Nagapattinam District, Tamil Nadu.

Objectives

The study aims at achieving the following objectives *viz.*,

1. to sketch the socio-economic origins of rural women entrepreneurs in study area.
2. to identify factors to choose entrepreneurship and problems of rural women entrepreneurs in promoting their business, and
3. to examine performance of group dynamics of SHGs.

Methodology

Sample Size. For the purpose of the study 31 rural women entrepreneurs were selected from SHGs *viz.*, Annai SHGs, Bharathi SHGs, Uthra SHGs, Sakthi SHGs and Shenbagam SHGs. The sample respondents *i.e.* 6 members from each have been selected on the basis of simple random sampling techniques in the study village. The relevant informations have been collected from both primary and secondary data.

Interview Schedule. Data have been obtained through personal interviews with the help of a pre-designed, field tested interview method. The investigator first developed an item pool based on the subject of the study. These items were given to experts for their opinion with regard to relevancy and adequacy for the conduct of the study. On the basis of suggestions from experts, some irrelevant items were dropped and others were modified. The questions on various aspects of the interview schedule were arranged in a sequential order and were administrated to a sample of 20 respondents for pretest. Based upon the pre-test, some of the questions were reordered and others modified to form the final interview schedule for the study.

RESULTS AND DISCUSSION

The present study, effort was made to present some important and interesting information pertaining to rural women entrepreneurship through SHGs in Mappadugai village, Mayiladuthurai T.K, Tamil Nadu. It was considered to evaluate the rural women entrepreneurs and a good deal of information concerning their socio-economic condition, problems in their businesses, group dynamic by them has been presented.

SOCIO-ECONOMIC PROFILE

Marital status of the rural women entrepreneurs indicated that majority of the rural women *i.e.* 95 percent are married. Actually there is no change in the unmarried categories but some of the married become destitute either widowed or divorced. Such happenings must have forced them to assume entrepreneurship.

Table 1. The Educational Details of the Sample Rural Women Entrepreneurs and Occupation

Education	Phenoil	Paper Cup	Draper	Phone Mat	Computer Sambirany	Total
Illiterate	1	—	1	1	—	3 (10%)
Primary	3	1	2	1	1	6 (20%)
Middle	1	2	1	1	1	6 (20%)
High School	—	2	—	3	1	6 (20%)
Higher Secondary	1	1	2	1	3	8 (24%)
Post Graduate	—	—	—	—	1	1 (3%)
Technical Diploma	—	1	—	—	—	1 (3%)

Source. Field Survey, 2006 Data.

The average size of the family has been 4 which tells that the size of the family is under control. Roughly 40 percent of them have more than four members in their families which may be joint families. Large size of the family also limits the contribution of the entrepreneurs to business to a great extent as these women need to devote most of their time on household activities.

Table 2. Age of the Sample Rural Women Entrepreneurs

Age Group	Phenoil	Paper Cup	Draper	Phone Mat	Computer Sambirany	Total
Below 20	—	—	—	—	—	
20–25	—	1	—	—	1	2 (7%)
26–30	1	—	—	1	1	3 (10%)
31–35	3	2	2	3	2	12 (40%)
36–40	2	3	3	1	1	10 (33.3%)
Above 40	—	—	1	1	1	3 (10%)

Source. Field Survey, 2006 Data.

The educational details of the sample rural women entrepreneurs explain that only 3 are illiterate. Another 24 percent respondents have higher secondary education. The educational details indicate that the majority of the sample entrepreneurs were not able to go for higher education but still were able to become entrepreneurs. This further indicates that education is not determining factor but only a facilitating factor.

The age distribution of the entrepreneurs explains that the maximum category entrepreneurs belonged to the age groups 31–35 years. This indicates that the women assume the entrepreneurs activity in the young age. This may be for two reasons. They might have been forced to assume due to poor economic conditions of the family. Another reason may be that these women entrepreneurs must have fulfilled the family requirements of child care.

Table 3. Compelling Factors to Choose to Entrepreneurship

Particulars	Score	Rank
Economic Compulsions	125	II
Education in the Line	30	VII
Expire/Inability of Parent/Husband	25	IX
Lot of Leisure Time Knowledge	60	III
Market and Techniques of Product	40	VI
Work Experience	45	V
Unemployment	150	I
Unemployment of Husband/Wife	30	VII
On the Job Training	20	X
Do not know Any Other Work	50	IV

Source. Field Survey, 2006 Data.

It is found in this present study that women took to entrepreneurship an account of unemployment and economic compulsion have forced. The other significant factors may include lot of leisure time, do not know any other work, work experience etc.

PROBLEMS FACED BY RURAL WOMEN ENTREPRENEURS

Financial Problems

The first problem faced by an rural woman entrepreneur is the procedural complications and problems with regard to surety, working capital and family support. The present research study found that among the rural women entrepreneur respondents chosen, the problem of surety gained the majority support of 70 percent while lack of family support scored the minimum of 30 percent only.

Rural Women Entrepreneurs faced on problems of Marketability of their products. The problems are arranged according to the percentage of strength as revealed by the survey results *viz.*,

(a) Managerial Constraints (5%)
(b) Lack of entrepreneurial initiative (5%)
(c) Problems of direct sale (60%)
(d) Storage facilities (10%)
(e) Role of intermediaries (10%)
(f) Competition from large scale (5%)

PROBLEMS OF RAW MATERIAL

Raw material plays an important role in small business because the availability and non availability of the raw material affects the functioning of the enterprise. 70 percent of sample women entrepreneurs reported that high price of raw material and the remaining said that competitions from large scale were the respective problems.

Social and Psychological Problems of Rural Women Entrepreneurs arouse due to

Gender bias: 50 percent of rural women entrepreneurs reported gender discrimination in the way of lack of motivation from family and society.

Feel like beings as women (15%)
Lack of confidence in women's ability (15%)
Inferiority complex (15%)
Lack of motivation (5%)
Non-co-operative attitudes of group members (–)

Rural Women Entrepreneurs Faced Problems Pertaining to Marketing Strategy

Sixty percent of the sample respondents have expressed lack of education—below higher secondary level.

Thirty percent of the sample States that there is lack of training and education could be imparted by the agencies both Government and private.

Among the General Problems Faced by Rural Women Entrepreneurs Activity Seems to be Based On

- **(a)** Excessive burden of work and responsibility (40%)
- **(b)** Health Problems (10%)
- **(c)** Lack of leisure time (20%)
- **(d)** Excessive tensions and Challenges (10%)
- **(e)** Lacks systematic planning and working (10%)
- **(f)** Poor risk taking ability (10%)

GROUP DYNAMICS OF RURAL WOMEN ENTREPRENEURS THROUGH SHGs

To what an extent do the respondents, responded to questions related to group cohesion which are shown in Table 4. An overwhelmingly large majority of 90 percent felt comfortable to work in their respective group. 85 percent were positive about the trust and confidence prevailing in the group and delegation of responsibility. 85 percent took part in group discussions.

Table 4. Group Dynamics Exhibited by the Members of SHGs

Aspects	Percentage of Respondents	
	Yes	No.
Feels Comfortable to Work in the Group.	90	10
Trust and Confidence Prevail in the Group.	85	15
Responsibilities Assigned Equally.	85	18
Participates in Group Discussions.	85	15
Disagreements Resolved in Democratic Ways.	90	10
Common Goals are set and Understood by Members.	90	10

Source. Field Survey, 2006 Data.

90 percent followed democratic way of their groups and 90 percent expressed that common goals are set and understood by members.

CONCLUSION

The present research study found that rural women entrepreneurs face several risks, most important among them are marketing and technological risks. Therefore, the development strategy for women entrepreneurship in rural areas should take these risks in to account while deciding opportunities. In fact the SHGs made a silent revolution in the rural womenfolk by enabling them to become self-dependent and self-reliant by accepting grassroots women entrepreneurship.

REFERENCES

- Anitha H. S. and Laximishra L. S. (1999) "***Women Entrepreneurship in India***" Southern Economist Vol. 38, No. 1.
- Chidambaram K. and Tenmozhi G. (1998) ***Constraints for Women Entrepreneurs***, Social Welfare Vol. 45, No. 1.
- David L. Lewis (1996), ***Understanding Rural Entrepreneurship in a Bangladesh Village Individual roles or structures Small Enterprise Development***, Vol. 7, No. 4.
- Manimekalai N (1999), ***Nature and Characteristics of Women Entrepreneurs in India***, in M.Soundarapandian (ed.), "***Women Entrepreneurship Issues and Strategies***," Kaniska Publishers, Distributors: New Delhi.
- Manimekali, N., and Ganesan., (2001) ***Global Women Entrepreneurs:AnAnalysis***, Southern Economist, July 15,2000.
- Lalitha., N., (2005) "***Women Entrepreneurs of Self Help Groups—A Case Study***"Journal of Extension and Research Vol. VII, No. 1&2.
- Shanta Kohli Chandr(1997), ***Development of Women Entrepreneurship***, Mittal Publications: New Delhi.
- Surekha Panandiker., (1985) "***Women Entrepreneurs : Problems and Potential***" Economic Times, December 26.
- Sivaloganation, K. (2002) "***Women Entrepreneurs—Problems and Prospects***"-Indian Economic Panorama Vol. 36, No. 6.

Grassroots Women Enterprenurship through SHGs

Financial Book—Keeping at a Self-Help Group in Study Village

Learning by Sharing Through SHGs in Study Village

Learning by Sharing Through SHGs in Study Village

Part—III

SHGs : Sectoral Studies

Chapter—13

Eradication of Poverty through SHGs : Vision 2020 (A Case Study of Assam)

—*Dr. Gautam Purkayastha**

> *"The poor need opportunity, not charity. The poor themselves can create a poverty-free world—all we have to do is to free them from the chains that we have put around them. Poverty is not created by the poor people. It is the institutions that we have built, and feel so proud of, which created poverty."*
>
> —*Prof. Mohumud Yunus*

INTRODUCTION

The credit needs of the poor are very small. Perhaps a loan worth Rs. 100 is enough to transform the life of a beggar (representing the most humiliated section of the society *i.e.*, the poorest of the poor). He/she can lead a responsible life as a newspaper hawker in a public place. Giving onetime hefty dole or occasional alms to the beggars may always

* Prof. & Head, Department of Economics, Margherita College, Margherita, Assam.

prove misdirected, a purely temporary exercise to reduce their sufferings. Apart from their access to kick-start capital, it is very important that they are being provided with right kind of information and necessary motivation which generally comes from voluntary organizations with professional skills/self-help groups (SHGs).

Credit is a major input in boosting economic development, only when it is effectively utilised. Its timely availability in the right quantity and at reasonable interest goes a long way in providing gainful economic activities in farm and non-farm sectors, particularly to the asset less poor. ***Hence two innovative schemes—micro credit through SHGs and entitlement to credit to all eligible people in the countryside through KCCs (Kisan Credit Cards)—were launched in Assam in the 1990s*** (along with the rest of the country) to eradicate perpetual mass poverty through self-employment and also to attain much faster economic growth.

ASSAM'S OVERALL ECONOMIC PERFORMANCE

As per Centre for Policy Alternative's recent report, 'Assam experienced growth rate of only 2.46 percent annually during the last decade as against 4.46 percent for NER's and 5.98 percent for India. The credit-deposit ratio was merely 28.95 percent in the State as compared to the national average of 59.37 percent as on March 31, 2003. All India Financial Institutions and Investment Companies are operating in the State, but there presence can be felt least in the region (Table 5 and 6—appendix). Consequently, centre's special economic packages could generate only a little response in the economy. Till recently, merely 2208 habitations out of the eligible 13144 habitations in the state have been connected under the schemes like PMGSY. Nearly 60 percent villages still lack all-weather connectivity. Most of the villages remain cut off from all marketing linkages during the long monsoon period of 4 to 6 months.

The Planning Commission's latest estimate shows that the incidence of poverty was very high in Assam, particularly in rural areas. Poverty estimates for the State of Assam in 1999–2000, on the basis of consumption expenditure data collected by NSSO (55th Round), indicate that 40.04% of rural population (over all—36.09%) was living under the poverty line. The corresponding national figures were 27.09 and 26.10 respectively. In absolute terms, nearly 10 million people constituting 3.63% of the poor Indians were living in Assam. The open unemployment in Assam accounted for 2 millions of which nearly 70 % were educated unemployed youths. Another 3 millions of the total work force were disguised unemployed, primarily engaged in the agricultural sector.

Providing employment to such a huge army of unemployed is a herculean task for the government. The possibility of absorbing a sizeable proportion of unemployed in different Government departments/defence sector is remote, because of the contractionist policy of the Government sector around the globe. Traditional agriculture cannot offer any additional (gainful) employment. The options left to the unemployed are in the modernization of the agricultural sector (diversification, sustainable mechanization and intensive use of the small holdings) and exploiting the untapped self-employment opportunities in the non-farm sectors including services (transport, health, education, etc.). One important solution to the above dismal picture surely lies in fostering SHGs among the disadvantaged people and involving NGOs (through a systematic institutional encouragement to them) in guidance and support services (*viz.*, finance management, enterprise development, packaging and pricing of products in consultation with expert teams studied with industrialists/industry managers) to the SHGs. The Government role should be restricted simply to a facilitator.

The current economic growth rate in the State is unsatisfactory. Population growth rate is still high. Moreover, there is a persistent threat of occasional spurts in infiltration of poverty ridden people from the neighbouring countries. Insurgencies are at large. Under such conditions, reduction of poverty in the State to half by next 10 years and below 10 percent level by 2020 warrants an all out efforts from all sections of the society in the areas of capacity building among the poor in backward areas.

MICRO FINANCE/MICRO CREDIT THROUGH SHGs

Micro finance comprises micro credit as well as savings products, pensions, payment services, housing loans, insurance, emergency and other private loans, etc. to poor and low income people and/or the enterprises they own. ***To bridge the wide gap between demand and supply of funds in the lower rungs of the rural economy, the formal sector took the initiative to develop a supplementary credit delivery mechanism by encouraging institutional arrangements outside the financial system. The above credit products can not be provided cost effectively by the banking system in isolation, in absence of NGOs/SHGs' cooperation and support.*** Consequently, as is clear from Table 1, at the all India level, 80% (even higher at 86% till March 2002—Table 2) of the total SHGs with linkages to banks received credit with NGOs' intermediation—financial or non-financial. In Assam, merely 6 percent of the total SHGs got credit from banks till March 2003. The role of NGOs in fostering SHG-bank linkages is still very much wanting in the State. The present dismal scenario of Assam

Table 1. SHG—Bank Linkage Patterns—All-India (March 2003)

	No. of SHGs	% Share
Model–I:	SHGs formed and financed by Banks	14266720
Model–II:	SHGs formed by NGOs & directly financed by Bank	51300572
Model–III:	SHGs financed by Banks through NGOs (on-lending)	616888

Cumulative as on March 31, 2003.

Source. Progress of SHG-Bank Linkage in India: 2002–03, NABARD, Mumbai, 2003.

can be changed substantially within a time bound period by facilitating the growth of competent NGOs and empowering the other agents of change in the society.

The conference of CEOs of Zila Parishads, BDOs and DRDA Project Directors, held at the Assam Administrative Staff College (Ist week of September, 2003) made an assessment of the SHGs, especially the factors retarding their growth. Lack of access to skill training, absence of market facilities, infrastructural bottlenecks, etc. were cited as the problem areas for the SHGs. It was also discussed with a note of concern ***that except those in Sonitpur District, none of the SHGs have received any sort of support from any NGO.***

Table 2. SHG—Bank Linkage Patterns—All-India (March 2002)

	No. of SHGs	% Share
Model–I:	SHGs formed and financed by Banks.	14% SHGs
Model–II:	SHGs formed by NGOs & directly financed by Banks.	70% SHGs
Model–III:	SHGs financed by Banks through NGOs (on-lending).	16% SHGs

Source. Financing Agriculture—in House Journal of Agricultural Finance Corporation Ltd., April–June, 2002.

MICRO CREDIT IN ASSAM

Individually poor households are considered as unbankable. However, in groups, poor households' credibility increases substantially to 'economically viable level.' ***In Assam, during the last 6 years or so (since 1999) nearly 1 lakh SHGs have been formed which covered roughly 60 lakh population. The State accommodates above 129 lakh population living at the subsistence level (including nearly poor population). Moreover, above one-half of the total SHGs were formed by the better off population and these groups constituted at least two-third of the State's SHG-Bank linkages.***

It seems that a mere 1/6th to 1/5th of the downtrodden in the state have come under group movement, which is a pre-requisite for the success of micro finance business and subsequently, eradication of poverty (Gautam Purkaystha, 2005). Indeed, the future task is very big. ***Still about 10 million people are needed to be motivated to pursue certain group activities for their socio-economic development. This demands, among others, large scale participation of PRIs and NGOs for capacity building particularly in rural areas.***

The growth in SHGs linked to banks in the NE-region/Assam was very low till the end of 2002. However, during 2003–04, SHG-bank linkages recorded an impressive 200 percent growth over the previous year as against the national average of 50 percent. Till March '04, in Assam, nearly 11000 SHGs got bank loans worth Rs. 16.86 crores.

NABARD had formulated a medium term strategy so as to cover one-third rural poor of Assam through credit linkage of about 48000 SHGs by March 2007. This is quite a reasonable target. It (NABARD) has to move very cautiously in the initial years in the sphere of facilitating credit-linkages, so that the in-built mechanism can easily identify/reach the target (interest) groups, while the opportunistic groups are screened out.

An all out effort is warranted from PRIs, NGOs and other catalyst agencies to change the dismal scenario in the State. ***When the state is reeling under poverty, unemployment and insurgencies, the poor involvement of banks in the rural market is a serious matter of concern.*** However, it is the responsibility of the catalyst agencies not to allow empowerment drive at the grassroots level goes waste like all other development drives of the past years by laying utmost priorities on capacity building of the SHG members, so that loan money can be circulated among an increasingly large number of SHGs. Most unfortunately, State's credit scenario is not yet as good as in the many other Indian States, even in the case of SHG and KCC loans.

Table 3. Performance of Micro Credit—1992–2004

Country/ State	SHG-Bank Linkage (Cumulative Progress)	Bank Loan (Crore)	Average Loan per SHG (Rs.)
All-India	10,79,091	3904.2	Rs. 3618
	6,11,043	2124.24 (Refinanced disbursed)	Rs. 3476
Assam	10708	16.85	Rs. 15747

Keeping in mind the fact that too small a loan can not generate sufficient income for a poor people to place him above the poverty line and also, fails to raise his repayment capacity, the total requirements of financial resources to allow access to livelihood finance (at the current price index) to all the needy households in Assam are estimated below:

Role of NGOs and Panchayats

As already mentioned ***micro credit cannot by itself eradicate poverty or assist in faster economic growth.*** 'Other financial and business services' must complement micro credits so as to make it work. Establishing connectivity/marketing linkages, proper identification of livelihood opportunities, upgradation of managerial and business skills and technical training of the poor, etc. are equally important issues which need to be looked into to foster micro credit as a strategy of poverty alleviation and development.

The impact assessment studies of micro-finance in India (MYRADA–NGO based in Bangalore; SHARE–NGO based in Hyderabad and BASIX–Non Banking Financial Company based in Andhra Pradesh) reported substantial reduction (38%–50%) of poverty among the SHG members. Other positive changes noted were improved self-confidence of the members, decision making in family affairs by women, decline in domestic violence (reported by 37%) including alcohol consumption and wife beating.

In an important assessment study carried out at Basix six years after inception, it was reported that ***'only 52 percent of our three-year plus micro credit customers reported an increase in income,*** 23 percent reported no change while another 25 percent actually reported a decline.' The reasons behind the poor performance were identified as follows:

- un-managed risk
- low productivity in crop cultivation and livestock rearing, and
- inability to get good prices from the input and output markets.

"Based on this study, Basix revised its strategy and now offers micro credit along with a whole suite of insurance products covering life, health, crop and livestock. For enhancing productivity, a whole range of agricultural and business development services are being offered to borrowers. For ensuring better prices, alternate market linkages are being facilitated both on the input and output side. Producers are encouraged to form groups and cooperatives, which

Table 4. Projected Population, BPL Population, SHGs and Microfinance in Assam

Current Population (2005):	2.86 Crore	Poor Population (30%)–	85.8 Lakh
(by simple aggregative method)		Nearly poor (15%)–	42.9 Lakh
		Total	128.7 Lakh
		Or, 26 Lakh poor households (Av. Size of the family = 5)	
Projected Population (2020):	3.75 Crore	Poor Population (10%)–	37.5
		Nearly poor (10%)–	37.5
		Total	75 Lakh
		Or, 15 Lakh poor households.	
1. Cumulative Micro Credit Requirements (including refinance) by 2020:		• Alternative Estimate for Micro Credit (MC) needs of the State (when access to the institutional credit for the poor is total).	
• 2004–10706 SHGs–	16.86 Crore		
• 2007–48000 SHGs–	96.00 Crore		
• (@ Rs. 20000 per group).		Total poor hhs: 26 Lakh.	
• 2010–80000 SHGs–	160 Crore	MC Requirements:	
• 2013–120000 SHGs–	240 Crore	(@ Rs. 5000 per hh): Rs. 1300 Crore.	
• 2016–150000 SHGs–	300 Crore	(@ Rs. 10000 per hh): Rs. 2600 Crore.	
• Refinanced disbural–	300 Crore		
• Total Cumulative MC Requirements by 2016/2020: (300 + 300) = 600 Crore			
2. Capacity building (assistance in group formation and recovery and delivery system); Rs. 30 Crores (5% of the Loan amount).		As per alternative estimate–	65 Crore
3. Connectivity: *Around 14000 villages need connectivity/better roads Rs. 7000 Crores (@1/2 Crore per village)			
4. Marketing linkages (Warehousing, cold storage, linkage to processing unit, better market information network) and allocation for integrated resource management: Rs. 60 Crores (10% of the Loan Amount)		Alternative estimate–	130 Crores.
5. Housing Loans/Assistance: Rs. 400 Crores (33% of the poor households @ Rs. 5000).			

* These figures are indicative. We need in-depth survey analysis in the above areas to estimate precise financial requirement for building basic infrastructures necessary for the success of Microfinance movement.

are then given institutional development services to become more effective." Institutional development services covered : ***formation and strengthening of various producer***

Table 5. State Wise and Population Group Wise Statement of Credit-Deposit Ratio of Banks in India: All Scheduled Commercial Banks (Credit-Deposit Ratio in Percentages)

Region/State	March 2001 Rural	March 2001 Urban/ Metropolitan	March 2001 Total	March 1994 Rural	March 1994 Urban/ Metropolitan	March 1994 Total
Northern Region	39.1	74.3	63.1	39.4	67.6	57.7
Haryana	41.9	43.8	41.4	51.0	51.3	47.9
Punjab	50.9	44.9	41.4	44.6	43.9	39.6
Rajasthan	47.6	56.7	48.2	54.0	52.4	49.2
Delhi	23.3	83.9	82.9	11.2	76.4	75.1
NE-Region	33.4	31.0	28.1	50.6	35.3	38.8
Arunachal Pradesh	18.8	—	17.3	14.1	—	14.1
Assam	34.4	39.3	32.4	56.4	39.8	41.2
Manipur	79.4	27.1	38.9	126.6	45.5	65.2
Meghalaya	22.9	15.7	16.8	33.0	13.8	17.3
Mizoram	61.1	16.1	25.5	39.2	—	24.5
Nagaland	33.1	—	13.9	52.7	—	42.0
Tripura	37.2	14.5	23.0	86.3	41.4	58.6
Eastern Region	25.9	47.1	36.9	48.5	47.3	44.0
Bihar	22.5	21.6	21.3	45.9	30.7	35.2
Orissa	42.6	45.0	41.5	71.9	56.8	60.0
West Bengal	23.4	52.7	44.1	43.1	50.4	45.9
Central Region	29.3	36.8	33.4	41.6	43.3	42.0
Madhya Pradesh	43.8	56.4	48.3	56.2	60.0	54.9
Uttar Pradesh	27.2	30.0	28.8	37.5	36.7	37.2
Western Region	48.4	83.2	75.0	46.9	55.9	53.2
Goa	12.6	—	22.8	11.2	—	18.1
Gujarat	38.0	58.5	49.4	45.5	48.9	46.0
Maharashtra	73.1	88.6	85.4	59.3	57.1	56.3
Southerr Region	67.1	76.5	65.8	75.8	69.0	67.3
Andhra Pradesh	77.4	64.4	63.3	82.6	73.9	70.7
Karnataka	68.5	58.9	59.3	72.9	68.0	65.6
Kerala	55.0	59.4	43.1	54.2	64.6	43.9
Tamil Nadu	59.6	109.0	90.6	82.7	89.1	82.4
All India	40.2	69.9	58.5	50.0	59.8	54.2

organizations such as self-help groups, water users' associations, forest protection committees, credit and commodity cooperatives, panchayats, etc. (EPW, October 8, 2005).

It seems that the concept micro finance covers a wide range of services. In absence of any of these services by the NGOs/ Panchayats, this relatively more effective poverty alleviation movement originated among the downtroddens may fail. This is more important in case of Assam where ***a large number of SHGs has come up under government's effort, by luring them with revolving fund and easy loan facilities*** (Gautam Purkayastha, 2005). Recent studies by CGAP show that only about a 100 of the 10000 odd microfinance institutions round the world are financially self-sufficient. This indicates that the general belief that micro credit can adequately serve the poor and in an economically viable manner is not well-grounded (at least in the initial years).

> According to NABARD data, by the end of the 1990s, about 800 NGOs were participating in its SHG-bank linkage programme. As regards emergence of NGOs as financial intermediaries (on-lending) or non-financial intermediaries (promoters of SHGs), the trend is positive. A study of 16 NGOs in Karnataka concluded that there is a mismatch between objectives and activities of these NGOs and the situation and needs of the poor with whom they work, but influenced by donor's priorities and policies (Rajasekhar 1998).

In Assam, only a few NGOs are working in this area. Most of them suffer from weak institutional capacities. Moreover, ***only a few NGOs are working with the poorest of the poor. Consequently, ex-tea communities and Muslim women remained largely uncovered by the current movement*** (Gautam Purkayastha, 2005).

Table 6. State Wise Average Recovery of Agricultural Loans and Credit Flow

State	Average Rate of Recovery	Agricultural Credit per Hectare of Net Sown Area (Rs.)
Northern Region		
Haryana	80	8611
Punjab	88	10786
Rajasthan	74	1167
North-Eastern Region		
Arunachal Pradesh	29	132
Assam	10	276
Manipur	11	115
Meghalaya	36	328
Mizoram	51	338
Nagaland	9	316
Tripura	32	481
Sikkim	NA	253
Eastern Region		
Bihar	26	572
Orissa	45	1269
West Bengal	61	1734
Central Region		
Madhya Pradesh	61	1104
Uttar Pradesh	66	2172
Western Region		
Gujarat	74	2887
Maharashtra	61	2363
Southern Region		
Andhra Pradesh	66	5253
Karnataka	62	3253
Kerala	83	9948
Tamil Nadu	70	7640
All India	63	—

Source. ECRC—2001, NABARD, Annexure 9.2.

FUTURE COURSE OF ACTION

— Attitude of the bankers needs to be changed on urgent basis. NGOs and PRIs' intermediation, pressure from other catalytic agencies, etc. can help a lot in this regard.

— Culture of repayment needs to be improved. In the author's one recent study (Gautam Purkayastha, 2005) it was found that as high as 48% of the institutional loans accumulated as overdues. Even in the case of bank loans to SHGs, the performance was found lower (<70%) than the national average of above 90 percent.

— Rate of interest charged by SHGs from the members (2–5% monthly) and non-members (2% to sometimes as high as 10%) should be made rational. Presently, many SHGs formed by the well-off members are engaged in usurious money lending business.

— Formation of the adequate number of NGOs in each District must receive due attention of the social institutions/higher educational institutions and also, of the policy makers (government). Provision of the meaningful training for capacity building of the NGOs, women organizations, Panchayats, etc. must receive utmost importance. In Assam, women organizations have a very large network which can be transformed into an effective and the largest NGO in the State by providing adequate amount of incentive, encouragement and training.

— It is estimated that if the Panchayats in Assam—with the help of women organizations and NGOs take up the responsibility to motivate at least 1 million poor a year to form groups for better utilization of their resources, only then, by 2016/2020, the problem of abject poverty can be addressed appropriately.

— Commercial Banks including RRBs, Cooperative Banks (which is presently in bad shape), NEDFi, SIRD, etc. must go ahead with a lot of determination to make a profit from lending to the poor. This demands putting considerable amount of energy for micro credit planning so that both ends gain and goals are achieved.

— Initially villages with better connectivity must be provided with micro credit services in adequate amount and only after improving basic infrastructures other villages should be brought under total coverage.

— SHGs and financial institutions must give priority to insurance of loan assets. This is very important as Concurrent Evaluation Study (July 1995–June 1996) revealed that in Assam, 52 percent IRDP beneficiaries were affected by natural calamities against all India average of 10 percent.

NOTES AND REFERENCES

- It can be noted that out of the 12136 organisations receiving foreign funding and reporting to the Home Ministry in 1996–97, there were 5721 organisations in south India alone, while the number was only 1779 in BIMARU region, thereby indicating that service delivery is taking place in the already better-off region while the poorer states are left out (Kulshrestha & Gupta, "NGOs in Micro Financing" Kurukshetra, February 2002).
- The source 'Gautam Purkayastha, 2005' refers to his post doctoral research project awarded by the UGC (still unpublished).
- In 2002–03, the author visited 16 villages in Assam—4 each in Kamrup, Karimganj, Nagaon and Tinsukia Districts—to collect primary data on rural credit pertaining to his Post-doctoral Research Project awarded by the UGC for a period of three years, 2002–2005. The author interviewed 500 households with due stress on spatial coverage of the State. The author observed the mushrooming growth of SHGs (the sample included 219 members from 179 SHGs/ 'credit and savings groups') in different parts of Assam, many of which cropped up just to get a

share in the Government distribution (Revolving Fund or subsidy based scheme) meant for the SHG-members.

- One encouraging finding of the study was that not a single SHG-member reported to have paid tips to the bank officials either for opening group account or getting the revolving fund and the loan amount released. This is no mean achievement. In the State of Assam almost all the individual beneficiaries under the government's subsidy driven loan schemes for self-employment required to pay at least some amount towards appeasement of the bank officials. This bad culture was considerably responsible for the state's poor repayment ratio (and consequently, low credit-deposit ratio).
- The study (Gautam Purkayastha, 2005) recommended that 'The present dismal scenario of Assam can be changed within a time bound period provided women organizations, teachers' associations, grassroots level developmental agencies including Panchayats, FMCs, NGOs and even religious institutions (like *Namghar*, etc.) come forward to act as financial or at least, non-financial intermediaries between banks and SHGs. For guidance and support services to the SHGs higher educational institutions may also be compulsorily encouraged by governments/ NABARD/SIRD so as to speed up the process of people orientation of the development strategy and fight against poverty.
- The report also cautioned that SHGs are much more than just financial mechanisms for extending micro credit to the poor for micro enterprises. Governments, NABARD, foreign donor's too much enthusiasm (target oriented approach) to promote and support a large number of SHGs always run the risk of transforming these groups into 'state-helped groups', thereby ruining their very foundation of self-help and autonomy of grassroots democratic organizations.

Chapter—14

Microfinance and Self-Help Groups—An Overview

—*Dr. A. Ramalingam**
—*S. Dharmaraj***

INTRODUCTION

India is one of the developing nations which has promoted institution for providing microfinance to the poor under various poverty alleviation programmes. Infact, India has the largest network branches in the world. Microfinance can be interpreted in a broader context; both micro credit and micro-finance have come to be used interchangeable.

* Reader in Economics, Post Graduate Research Department of Economics, A.V.C. College (Autonomous), Mannanpandal, Mayiladuthurai, Tamil Nadu.

** Ph.D. Scholar, Post Graduate and Research Department of Economics, A.V.C. College (Autonomous), Mannanpandal, Mayiladuthurai, Tamil Nadu

MICROFINANCE

Microfinance means providing very poor families with small loan (micro credit) to help them engage in productive activities or grow their tiny business. It plays an important role in the fight against the many aspects of poverty.

Microfinance through Self-Help Groups has emerged as a catalyst to help meet the credit needs of informal or unorganised rural sector in the recent past. This has necessitated a shift of strategy from priority sector lending to Self-Help Groups to micro credit and now Microfinance. The Reserve Bank of India has initiated a few steps to encourage Bank lendings to SHGs as a part of a mainstream banking activity. Credit extended by Commercial Banks to SHGs is treated as part of priority sector lending in order to encourage banks to engage in this sort of activity. Banks have also been bestowed procedures and design loan products for SHGs responding to local conditions.

In India, efforts are made to promote Microfinance in a sustainable manner. As important vehicle for this has been the Self-Help Groups (SHGs) programme and its linkage with Banks.

SELF-HELP GROUPS

Self-Help Groups (SGHs) is defined as a "self governed, peer controlled informal group of people with similar socio-economic background and having a desire to collectively perform common purpose."

It is a homogeneous group of poor people voluntarily coming under—to save whatever amount they can conveniently out of their earnings, to mutually agree to contribute, to a common fund and to lend to the numbers for meeting their productive and emergent needs.

The funds thus created are used for giving loans to its members. Such loan include, ***consumption loans*** and

production loans. The consumption loans include subsistence needs, health care, social and religious ceremonies etc., The production loans are for the purpose of purchase of agricultural inputs, investment on poultry, sheep and for small business like vending, hawking, etc.

MICROFINANCE AND ECONOMIC EMPOWERMENT OF SHGs

Majority of people in India live in the rural areas and earn their livelihood from agriculture related activities. The major challenge before the nation today is to evolve an appropriate strategy for mobilising the human resources for optimising use of the available financial resources. The concept of Microfinance was introduced for overcoming the existing constraints and providing adequate credit to the poor in general and the weaker section in particular by following a simple procedure.

National level corporations like National Scheduled Caste Finance and Development Corporation (NSFDC), National Safai Karmachari Finance and Development Corporation (NSKFDC), National Backward Classes Finance and Development Corporation (NBCFDC) and National Minorities Development and Finance Corporation (NMFDC) set up in India, were directed recently for meeting the smaller loan requirements at a lower rate of interest than that charged by Banks, covering the target groups belonging to scheduled castes and Scheduled Tribes and other Backward Classes, Minorities and Safai Karamcharis. The coverage of beneficiaries by these corporations has seen a quantum jump during 2000–01 and 2001–02 following adoption of Microfinance. These corporations took several specific steps for facilitating provision of Microfinance, such as:

(i) Liberalisation of procedures for sanctioning the loan initially and repeating it subsequently;

(ii) Delegation of power to the Managing Director for sanctioning the loan;

(iii) Introducing provision of Revolving Fund (upto Rs. 25 lakhs) for assisting reputed Non-government organization having previous experience in the field of Microfinance;

(iv) Liberalizing rate of interest (at rate not exceeding 10% from the beneficiary, of which 6% is passed to the NGO and SHGs.

(v) Support for capacity building measurer like organization of training, workshop; and

(vi) For marketing their products by participating in fairs etc.

These corporations offering institutional sources of micro credit are successful in mobilising women groups and providing them training as well as financial assistance for preparation of food, purchase of equipments like utensils, gas stoves, pressure cooker, tiffin carriers and working capital, assistance to artisans engaged in wood-carving and brass inlay, and also assistance for rehabilitation of Tribal women and Devdasis, for promoting dairy and handloom activities, for purchase of raw materials and also for financing the purchase of cattle and training for dry flower arrangements. These corporations are helpful in meeting the credit needs of the small households and enabling them to cross poverty line by supplementing their income substantially and acquisition of assets to some extent.

Microfinance has become a part of the lending pattern of Banks in India for providing credit to very small borrowers who normally remain beyond the reach of institutional credit agencies.

"A Self-Help Group is a registered or unregistered group of micro entrepreneurs with a homogeneous social and economic background, voluntarily coming together to save small amounts regularly and mutually agreeing to contribute to a common fund to meet their emergency needs on mutual help basis. The group members use collective wisdom and peer pressure to ensure proper end-use of credit and timely repayment thereof." In the ***evolution of Microfinance*** industry there are five models based on different philosophies and target groups. They are:

(i) Grameen and solidarity model developed in Bangladesh and now popular in South Asia.

(ii) SHGs model popular in India, Indonesia and Kenya.

(iii) Individual credit—mostly priority sector lending in India.

(iv) Community Banking Developed in Latin America and replicated in Africa and Central Asia.

(v) Credit Unions and cooperatives popular in Sri Lanka.

The high powered task force set up by NABARD in November 1998 has defined Microfinance as "provision of thrift, credit and other financial services and products of very small amounts to the poor in rural, semi-urban or urban areas for enabling them raise their income levels and improve living standards" and "Microfinance Institutions (MFIs) as those which provide thrift, credit, and other financial services and products for the above."

Hence, Microfinance focused on providing a very standardized credit product to the poor just like anyone else, have a diverse range of economical instrument to be able to build assets normal consumption and guard themselves against financial risks.

Economic Empowerment is the initial aspect of woman development. It means, greater access to financial resources inside and outside the household reducing vulnerability of poor women crisis situation like, famine, flood, riots, death or accidents in the family.

Economic Empowerment gives women the power to retain income and use it at her discretion. Financial self reliance of women both in the household and in the external environment lead to empowerment of women in other spheres. The economic empowerment provides income security possession of ownership of productive assets and developing entrepreneurship skill.

The 63 percent of total credit availed by the rural poor is used for consumption purposes with only 37 percent going to productive use. Then the overall share of organized sector in credit flow to the rural poor is around 16 percent.

Till march 2002, Banks in India financed 4.61 lakh SHGs of them 90 percent were SHGs comprising only women. The most encouraging future was that timely repayment of loans consistently remained at over 65 percent although ready 85 percent of SHGs members were first time borrowers.

BANK LINKAGE PROGRAMME IN INDIA

An important milestone in this direction is the NABARD's SHGs—Bank linkage programme started in 1991. The NABARD's SHGs Bank linkage Programme helps to meet the credit needs of the poor by combining the flexibility, sensitivity and responsiveness of the informal credit system with the strength of technical, administrative capabilities and

Table 1. SHGs Bank Linkage Programme in India

Year	No. of SHGs Financed (in Thousands)	No. of Families Assisted (in Thousands)	Bank Loan Rs. in Crore	Average Loan per SHG (Rs.)	Average Loan per Family (Rs.)
1992–93	0.22	4.33	0.30	11765	692
1995–96	2.63	44.80	3.6	13700	806
2000–01	149.05	2533.25	287.89	10315	1136
2003–04	361.73	5425.00	1862.00	51474	3431
2004–05	518.71	7774.00	2961.80	57099	3869
Cumulative as on 31.3.05	1597.80	23960.00	6866.00	42971	2865

Source. NABARD Progress and Perspectives of SHGs in Karnataka, 2003–04.

financial resources of the formal finance institution. The SHGs, NABARD made it a tremendous success. There are 714.000 SHGs that are linked to banking system today. What is important is that over one crore women has emerged as beneficiary of this scheme. The progress of SHGs Bank linkage is given Table 1.

The major institutional initiatives include the SHGs-Bank Linkage Programme under the overall guidance and supervision of the NABARD. The setting up of the Rastriya Mahila Kosh to refinance microfinance activities of the NGOs and the establishment of SIDBI foundation for micro credit as a financier of Microfinance institutions. The policy front the RBI has given directives that classified lending to SHGs as a part of priority sector lending. There have been many fiscal initiatives too both from the Central and many State Governments. The Swaranjayanti Gram Swarozgar Yojana (SGSY) and Swa-Skakti— a Central Government Scheme exclusively targeting rural women are routed through the SHGs.

CONCLUSION

The Self-Help Groups (SHGs) are the latest breeds of the Microfinance in India. The SHGs proved beyond doubt that they are the fastest growing and most effective micro financial initiatives in the Indian context. It would provide information for improving their capacity for productivity and it would also help women to attain their income security. Hence, the idea of Microfinance is simple. If poor people are provided access to financial services, including credit they may very well be able to start or expand a micro-enterprise that will allow them to break out poverty and pave for the economic empowerment of women.

REFERENCES

- S. K. Nashi "***Microfinance : A Study of Shree Shakti (SHGs) Programmes***", ***Southern Economist***, Vol. 43, No. 8, August, 15, 2004. p. 7.

- *Reserve Bank of India* 2002–03, Sep.–2003, p. 143.
- ***Reserve Bank of India Report*** on Trend and Progress of Banking in India 1999–2000, December 2000, p. 123.
- M. S. Chandrakavate, "***The SHGs Model of Microfinance : A Silent Movement towards Empowering Rural Women*, *Southern Economist***, Vol. 44, No. 77, January 1, 2006.

Chapter—15

Credit Utilization Pattern of Self-Help Group Members

—Prof. V. Sekar*
—G. Narayanan**
—V. Saravanakumar***

INTRODUCTION

The Self-Help Group (SHG) movement in Tamil Nadu made a humble beginning in 1989 as International Federation for Agricultural Development (IFAD) assisted pilot project in two blocks in Dharmapuri District. By realizing the potentialities of this SHG, the Tamil Nadu Government initiated an ambitious programme termed as "Mahalir Thittam" with the intention to reach the poorest among the poor in all community and with much emphasis on Scheduled Caste and Scheduled Tribes. Beyond

* Prof. and Head, Department of Social Sciences, Horticultural College Research Institute, Periyakulam, Tamil Nadu.
** Ph.D. Scholar, IARI, New Delhi.
*** Teaching Assistant, Department of Social Sciences, Horticultural College Research Institute, Periyakulam, Tamil Nadu.

the expectation of Tamil Nadu Government, this programme made a strong root in rural society and spread throughout the State within a short span.

The Self-Help Group is a substantial approach to make credit facilities available to the poor at their door step in a simple and flexible manner. The SHGs are being linked with the Banks for the external credit under the projects of rural development officers. NGOs project implementation units visit the group and select the beneficiaries proposed by women groups for providing financial assistance to the respective entrepreneurial activities.

The NGOs have very significant role to play in and out activities of SHGs. The NGOs with considerable history of working in a particular area for projects like literacy, sanitation etc., organize SHGs, bringing together people, explaining the concept to them, attending and helping to co-ordinate a few of the initial group meetings, helping them to maintain accounts and linking them with the Banks. Some of the Rural Bank themselves are being designated as Self-Help Group Promoting Institution (SHGPI) and they help in the formation and nursing of SHGs.

As per the report of Tamil Nadu Corporation for Women Development (TNCWD) Chennai 2003, there are 1,42,682 SHGs, with an enrollment of 2,427,141 women in Tamil Nadu under Mahalir Thittam.

This SHG approach has been taken up by the women as one of the viable ways to achieve their empowerment. This made them to get free from the clutches of moneylenders in one hand and on the other hand helps them to stand on their own legs within the family. Apart from these benefits, this SHG approach made the rural women to participate in literacy, health and socio-economic programmes which they were not endowed to do so. Hence, in nutshell it can be say that the SHG movement made an impact not only on empowerment of women through entrepreneurial activities but also made great impact in family, community and nation as a whole in this decade. Keeping the above facts in mind a research was carried out with the following specific objectives.

The Specific objectives of the study were:

1. To study the credit utilization pattern of Self-Help Groups,
2. To analyze the relationship between credit utilization pattern and characteristics of Self-Help Group members, and
3. To know the constraints faced by the group members and suggest suitable remedial measures to overcome the same.

This study was conducted in six villages of Vadipatti Block of Madurai District in Tamil Nadu with the sample size of 120 SHG members who were drawn through random sampling technique. Data collected through pre-tested and well structured interview schedule were properly interpreted by using suitable statistical tools such as percentage, regression, correlation, path analysis, cumulative frequency etc. The findings of the research are presented below.

CREDIT UTILIZATION PATTERN OF SHG MEMBERS

This refers to utilization of credit by the SHG members, the purpose for which they obtained credit. It is believed that among the beneficiaries some of the members also utilized money for other than the entrepreneurial purpose.

Hence to find out the percentage of amount utilized for economic activities from the borrowed amount the data were collected and the results are furnished in Table 1 and Fig 1.

It could be inferred from the Table 1 that majority (80.00 percent) of the members utilized the borrowed amount for entrepreneurial purposes. Among them 60.84 percent of SHG members fully utilized and 19.16 percent

Table 1. Distribution of Respondents According to their Credit Utilization Pattern

(n = 120)

Category	Number	Percent
Loan Amount fully Utilized for Entrepreneurial Purpose	73	60.84
Loan Amount Partially Utilized for Entrepreneurial Purpose	23	19.16
Loan Amount Utilized for Non-Entrepreneurial Purposes	24	20.00
Total	120	100.00

partially the loan amount for entrepreneurial activities. However 20.00 percent of the members utilized the borrowed amount for non-entrepreneurial activities such as clearing

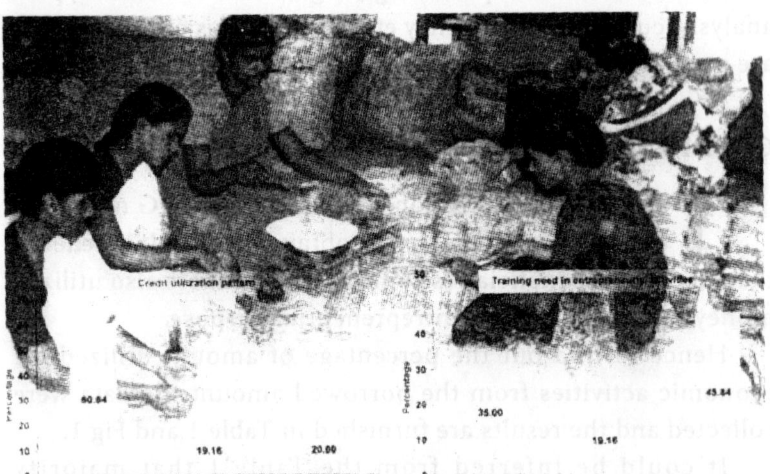

Fig. 1. Distribution of Responents According to their Credit Utilization Pattern and Training Needs in Entrepreneurial Activities.

of old debts, food, health care, children's education and for religious and social ceremonies. This result is in accordance with the result of Renganathan (2001). He also reported that cent percent of Pradhan Mantri Rozgar Yojana (PMRY) beneficiaries were utilized the credit for the intended purpose.

Further an attempt also made to know the utilization of credit for the various entrepreneurial activities and the results are presented in Table 2.

Table 2. Distribution of SHG Members According to their Involvement in Entrepreneurial Activities

(n = 120)

Entrepreneurial Activities	Number	Percent
Dairy Farming	72	60.00
Goat and Sheep Rearing	0	0.00
Establishment of Poultry Unit	0	0.00
Mushroom Cultivation	0	0.00
Grocery Shop—Petty Shop	6	5.00
Vegetable Vending	0	0.00
Rice Sales	2	1.66
Masala Preparation	2	1.66
Snacks Preparation	6	5.00
Preparation of Jam, Juice, Pickles	0	0.00
Preparation of Appalam, Vadagam	3	2.53
Tailoring Unit	0	0.00
Opening of Mini Hotel	2	1.66
Sambirani, Agarpathi Production	2	1.66
Simple Chemicals Production	1	0.83
Non-Entrepreneurial Activites	24	20.00
Total	120	100.00

SELF-HELP GROUP MEMBERS INVOLVEMENT IN ENTREPRENEURIAL ACTIVITIES

Women in the Self-Help movement have slowly and steadily got involved in micro level enterprises with the support of credit institutions. Now the women are coming out from their traditional homebound works to marketing their goods and wares. They are courageously trying to stand on their own legs with help of credit institutions in their traditionally male dominated society.

The study area too the women are involved in innovative economic activities such as dairy farming, goat and sheep rearing, establishment of poultry unit, mushroom cultivation, establishment of grocery shop-petty shop, vegetable vending, rice sales, masala preparation, snacks and pickles production, preparation of jam and juice, preparation of appalam, vadagam, starting tailoring unit, starting mini hotel, preparation of sambirani and agarpathi, production of phenoil, cleaning powder and bleaching powder with the financial assistance of credit institutions.

Hence an attempt has been made in the study to know the involvement of SHG members in various entrepreneurial activities and the results are furnished in Table 2.

The Table 2 implies that majority (60.00 percent) of the Self-Help Group members are taking up dairy farming, which is remained the more favourable income generating activities among the members. Further they could sell milk in the local milk co-operatives and also preparing value added products such as ghee, butter, butter milk, and milk based sweets (Fig.2)

Establishing grocery/petty shop and preparation of snacks have been taken up as entrepreneurial activities by 5.00 percent of SHG members. Very few were involved in entrepreneurial activities like selling of rice, preparation of masala, appalam, vadagam, sambirani, agarpathi and simple chemicals.

Therefore it may be concluded that majority of the SHG members could not able to divert themselves from home based enterprises such as dairy farming to other economic activities due to lack of knowledge and skill to do the practices.

CONTRIBUTION OF CHARACTERISTICS TOWARDS CREDIT UTILIZATION PATTERN

Correlation will explain only the nature of association between the characteristics of the SHG members and credit utilization pattern. In order to find out the relative contribution of each variable towards credit utilization pattern multiple regression analysis was performed and the results are presented in Table 3.

It could be discerned from the Table 3 that the R_2 value was 0.501 that indicated that 50.10 percent of variation in credit utilization pattern of SHG members was explained by seventeen variables selected for the study. The '*F*' value 5.912 was significant at one percent level of probability. The prediction equation for the cause and effect relationship was fitted for the credit utilization pattern of the SHG members as given below. There existed a linear functional relationship between the independent variables and dependent variable.

The Table 3 indicated that regression co-efficient of five variables *viz.*, age, socio-economic status, achievement motivation, credit orientation and self-confidence was positively significant at one percent level of probability. Risk orientation was negatively significantly at one percent level of probability:

$$
\begin{aligned}
Y_1 = & -103.821 + 0.803^{**}X_1 - 0.581\,X_2 - 1.760\,X_3 \\
& + 4.408)4 + 4.181\,X_5 + 1.265\,X_6 + 1.754\,X_7 + 2.387\,X_8 \\
& + 3.482^{**}X_9 - 0.369\,X_{10} - 1.235^{**}\,X_{11} \\
& + 1.541^{**}X_{12} + 1.518\,X_{13} + 4.429^{**}X_{14} \\
& + 1.131^{*}\,X_{15} + 257\,X_{16} + 0.168\,X_{17}
\end{aligned}
$$

Table 3. Association and Contribution of Characteristics with Credit Utilization Pattern of SHG Members

(n = 120)

Variable Number	Variables	Correlation Co-efficient	Partial Regression Co-efficient	Standard Error	't' Value
X_1	Age	0.1418NS	0.803	0.285	3.371**
X_2	Educational Status	0.2539**	–0.581	–0.022	–0.220
X_3	Nature of Family	0.1305NS	–1.760	–0.041	–0.502
X_4	Nature of House Owned	0.2292*	4.408	0.151	1.578
X_5	Occupation	0.2367**	4.181	0.103	1.198
X_6	Material Possession	0.2749**	1.265	0.035	0.341
X_7	Caste	0.2721**	–1.754	–0.062	–0.649
X_8	Social Participation	0.2822**	2.387	0.117	1.487
X_9	Socio-Economic Status	0.5099**	3.482	0.393	2.727**
X_{10}	Localiteness-Cosmopoliteness	0.1043NS	–0.369	–0.084	–1.030
X_{11}	Risk Orientation	–0.0745NS	–1.235	–0.213	–2.654**
X_{12}	Achievement Motivation	0.2030*	1.541	0.225	2.956**
X_{13}	Economic Motivation	0.3085**	1.518	0.081	0.918
X_{14}	Credit Orientation	0.1162NS	4.429	0.219	2.612**
X_{15}	Self-Confidence	0.3513**	1.131	0.217	2.333*
X_{16}	Training Undergone	0.1932*	–0.257	–0.009	–0.107
X_{17}	Attitude Towards Group Activity	–0.0239NS	0.168	0.011	0.136

* Significant at Five Percent Level. **Significant at One Percent Level. $R^2 = 0.501$ $F = 5.912^{**}$

This indicates that a unit increase *ceteris paribus* in socio-economic status (X_9), achievement motivation (X_{12}), credit orientation (X_{14}), and self-confidence (X_{15}) would result in an increase of 3.482, 1.541, 4.429 and 1.131 units respectively. A unit increase *ceteris paribus* in nature of family (X_3) caste (X_7), risk orientation (X_{11}) would result in decrease of 1. 760, 1.754, 1.235 units respectively.

Hence, it could be inferred from the study that credit utilization pattern of members of SHGs would have positively influenced by socio-economic status, achievement motivation, credit orientation and self-confidence. On the other hand the credit utilization patterns of the SHG members were negatively influenced by the variables such as nature of family, caste and risk orientation.

From the study it may be concluded that the SHG members with high level of Socio-economic status, credit orientation and self-confidence tend to have high level of utilization of credit.

Direct, Indirect and Substantial Effects of Independent Variables on Credit Utilization Pattern of the SHG Members

Credit utilization has been associated with a number of variables as discussed elsewhere. But these variables themselves might be interrelated. Such interdependence of those variables, affect the contributory factors having the direct relationship with the credit utilization pattern, thus by making the correlation co-efficient as unreliable indices. Path analysis permits the separation of direct effects and indirect effects through the other variables by apportioning the correlation co-efficient. Hence an attempt has been made to evaluate the association of credit utilization pattern and of the other selected significant variables through path analysis. The results are given in Table 4.

Table 4. Direct, Indirect and Substantial Effects of Independent Variables on Credit Utilization Pattern of SHG Member

(n = 120)

Variable Number	Variables	Direct	Indirect	Substantial Effects I	II	III
X_1	Age	0.2727	–0.1309	0.0808 (X_{12})	–0.0775 (X_9)	0.0387 (X_{11})
X_2	Educational Status	–0.0533	0.2819	0.2249 (X_9)	0.0762 (X_{12})	0.0692 (X_{15})
X3	Nature of Family	–0.0399	0.1704	0.1109 (X_9)	0.0757 (X_{12})	0.0446 (X_{15})
X_4	Nature of House Owned	0.1412	0.0871	0.1003 (X_9)	–0.0350 (X_{11})	–0.0248 (X_{12})
X_5	Occupation	0.1001	0.1365	0.1806 (X_9)	0.0347 (X_4)	–0.0307 (X_3)
X_6	Material Possession	0.0192	0.2557	0.2190 (X_9)	–0.0381 (X_2)	–0.0303 (X_3)
X_7	Casts	–0.0807	0.3367	0.2338 (X_9)	0.0551 (X_{12})	0.0400 (X_{15})
X_8	Social Participation	0.1241	0.1582	0.1114 (X_9)	0.0331 (X_{11})	0.0254 (X_{15})
X_9	Socio-Economic Status	0.4255	0.0844	0.0738 (X_{12})	0.0568 (X_{15})	–0.0497 (X_1)
X_{10}	Localiteness-Cosmopolitenes	–0.0879	0.1921	0.1440 (X_9)	0.0275 (X_{14})	–0.0217 (X_1)
X_{11}	Risk Orientation	–0.2105	0.1360	0.0646 (X_{12})	0.0503 (X_9)	–0.0501 (X_1)
X_{12}	Achievement Motivation	0.2526	–0.0496	0.1242 (X_9)	–0.0538 (X_{11})	–0.0872 (X_1)
X_{13}	Economic Motivation	0.0870	0.2215	0.1106 (X_{15})	0.1027 (X_9)	0.0386 (X_{12})
X_{14}	Credit Orentation	0.2141	–0.0978	0.0487 (X_{11})	–0.0220 (X_{11})	–0.6216 (X_4)
X_{15}	Self-Confidence	0.2222	0.1291	0.1037 (X_9)	–0.0474 (X_{11})	0.0450 (X_{12})
X_{16}	Training Undergone	–0.066	0.1998	0.1116 (X_9)	0.0328 (X_4)	–0.0664 (X_{11})
X_{17}	Attitude Towards Group Activity	–0.0016	–0.0223	–0.0714 (X_1)	0.0603 (X_9)	0.0341 (X_3)

It could be seen from the Table 9 that the independent variables namely Socio-economic status (X_9), achievement motivation (X_{12}), Age (X_1), Self-confidence (X_{15}), Credit orientation (X_{14}) were having high direct effect on credit utilization pattern. While variables namely nature of houses owned (X_4), social participation (X_8) and occupation (X_5) had shown lower direct effect.

Out of indirect effects studied, socio-economic status (X_9) showed a dominating role since fifteen variables passed through it. Achievement motivation (X_{12}) ranked second since twelve variables had passed through it. Risk orientation (X_{11}) ranked third since seven variables had passed through it. Self-confidence (X_{15}) ranked fourth since six variables had passed through it. Age (X_1) ranked fifth since four variables passed through it. The independent variables nature of house owned (X_4) and nature of family (X_3) are ranked sixth since three variables each had passed through it. The independent variable educational status (X_2) ranked seventh since one variable had passed through it.

It could be concluded from the path values that the variables socio-economic status, achievement motivation, age, self-confidence, credit orientation had higher direct effects on credit utilization pattern of members of SHGs. With respect to substantial effect socio-economic status, achievement motivation, risk orientation and self-confidence were observed to have dominating effects towards the credit utilization pattern.

Constraints Faced by the Self-Help Group Members in Participation of Entrepreneurial Activities

The constraints faced by the SHG members in the participation of entrepreneurial activities are presented in Table 5.

Table 5. Constraints Faced by the SHG Members in Participation of Entrepreneurial Activities

(n = 120)

Constrains	Number	Percent
Domestic Work and Child Care Problems	71	59.17
Lack of Co-operation from Husband and Elderly Members of the Family	66	55.00
Lack of Marketing for SHG Products	66	55.00
No Awareness about Credit Management and Records Maintenance by Leaders	48	40.00
Training Centers are far away from Native	46	38.33
Formation of Groups based on Caste	33	27.50
Lack of Effective Leadership	16	13.34
Lack of Co-operation among SHG Member in the Group	8	6.67

(Multiple Responses Obtained)

From the Table 5 it could be observed that domestic work and child care problems were expressed as constraints by majority (59.17 percent) of SHG members. Because of domestic work and child care problem, the SHG members were unable to spent time to participate in SHG activities. This is one of the most important problems for low participation of SHG members in development activities.

Just more than half (55.00 percent) of the SHG members were expressed as lack of marketing for their products. Lack of encouragement from husband and other members of the family as one of the constraints for effective functioning SHGs. The members expressed that their family members did not support and allow them to participate in SHG activities.

About 40.00 percent of respondents revealed that the improper repayment and lack of awareness about credit management as the constraints, whereas 38.33 percent of respondents felt no sharing of domestic work by family members and also the training centre is far away from the native place.

Formation of groups based on caste was expressed as one of the constraints by 27.50 percent of SHG members. It was learnt that since the majority of the members were belonged to Backward Community the suggestions given by the scheduled caste members were not taken into account.

Lack of effective leadership was expressed as one of the constraints by 13.34 percent of the SHG members. It was observed during the survey that during meeting the actual leader was not participated but the responsibilities of leader was delegated to cashier or relatives of the leader. Only 6.67 percent of the SHG members were expressed lack of co-operation among the SHG members in the group as their constraints for effective participation in SHG activities.

Suggestions given by the SHG members for Effective Participation in SHG Activities

The suggestions expressed by SHG members for effective participation in SHG activities were collected and presented in Table 6. This section deals with suggestions that would enable the respective authorities to take required steps, so as to solve their problems and ultimately increase their effective participation in development activities of their own village.

About 65.00 percent of the SHG members suggested that domestic work and child care should be shared by the family SHG members to reduce their work load in home activities and to solve day-to-day problems and child care activities.

Above half (58.33 percent) of the respondents suggested that they could participate in SHG activities if the family members could provide support and encourage the SHG members to participate.

It is understood from the Table 6 that little above half (55.00 percent) of the SHG members suggested that necessary support is needed from Government and NGO for starting of SHG stores.

Table 6. Suggestions given by the SHG Members for Effective Participation in SHG Members

(n = 120)

Constrains	Number	Percent
Family Members Should Share Domestic Work and Childcare	78	65.00
Family Members Should Support and Encourage the SHG Members to Participate in SHG Activities	70	58.33
Market Facility is Necessary for Selling the SHG Products	66	55.00
Training should be Organized within the Village	53	44.16
Leader should be Selected based on their Experience, Planning and Supervision Qualities	20	16.67
Formation of Caste based Groups Should be Strictly Avoided.	15	12.50
Members should give Co-operation to their Group Members	8	6.67

(Multiple Responses Obtained)

It could be inferred from the Table that majority (44.16 percent) of respondents preferred that the training should be organized within their village.

About 16.67 percent of the SHG members were suggested that the leader should be selected based on their experience, planning and supervision qualities.

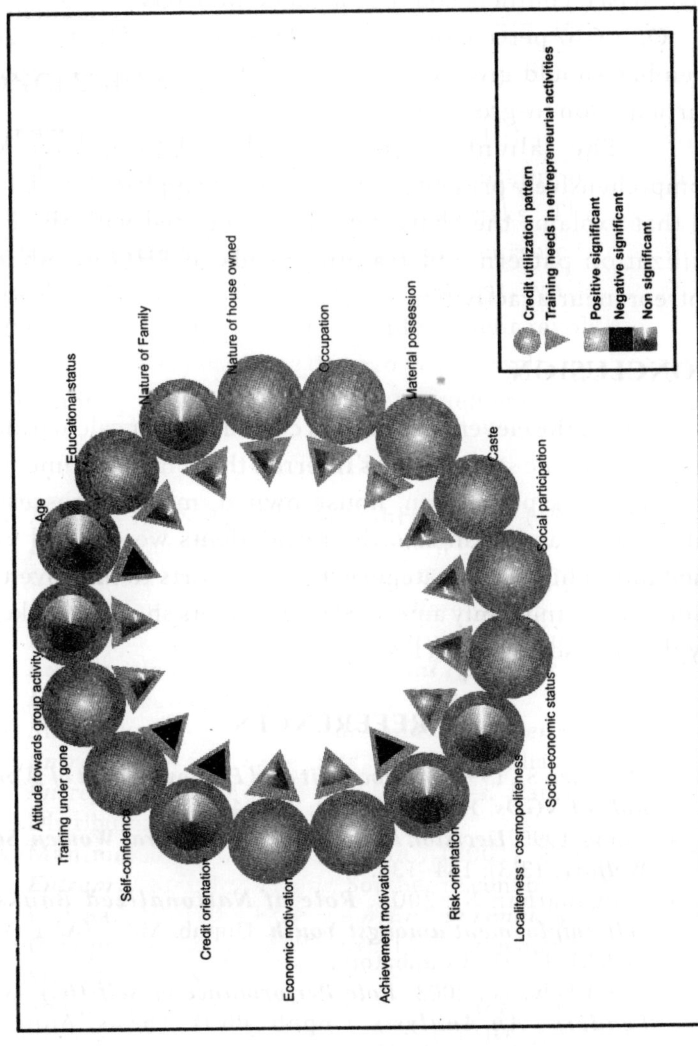

Fig 2. Empirical Model Showing the Relationship between Independent and Dependent Variables.

Formation of groups based on caste should be avoided was the suggestion given by 12.50 percent of respondents. So that caste based conflicts could be avoided in SHGs.

Only 6.67 percent of SHG members expressed that the group member should give co-operation to their group for effective participation in-group activities.

The salient outcomes of this chapter have been comprehensively presented in the form of empirical model (Fig. 3) that explains the characteristics associated with the credit utilization pattern and training needs of SHG members in entrepreneurial activities.

CONCLUSION

Among the eleven dimensions considered for calculating the socio-economic status, it was inferred that only the dimensions *viz.*, livestock possession, house owned, material possession, farm power and farm size the respondents were found under medium to high level category. Hence, efforts to improve these dimensions uniformly among SHG members should be taken up by the sponsoring agencies.

REFERENCES

- Mohanan S., 1999. ***Microcredit and Empowerment of Women-Role of NGOs, Yojana***, 44(11): 21–24.
- Pande, 1995. ***Decision Making Pattern of Rural Women, Social Welfare***, 13(3): 134–138.
- Renganathan S., 2001. ***Role of Nationalized Banks for Self-employment amongst Youth***. Unpub. M.Sc. (Ag.) Thesis, AC&RI, TNAU, Coimbatore.
- Tamil Selvi G., 2003. ***Role Performance of Self-Help Group Leaders—An Analysis.*** Unpub. Ph.D. Thesis, Annamalai University, Annamalai Nagar.
- Fernandez A. P., 1995. ***Self Help Groups—The Concept, Mysore Rehabilitation Development Agency***; 1–15.

- Mohanthy M., 1997. "***Decision-making in Home and Farm Related Activities***," Kurukshetra, 43(11) : 30--37.
- Radharani N. and A. Laxmidevi, 1992. "***Problems of Biogas Beneficiaries***," ***Indian Journal of Extension Education***, 28 (3 and 4) : 44–48.
- Sujatha, Jane, J., 1996. ***Gender Analysis in different Farming Systems***, Unpublished Ph.D. Thesis, Tamil Nadu Agricultural University, Coimbatore.
- Velusamy R., 1996. ***Impact of Non-governmental Organizations in Rural Development***, Unpublished M.Sc. (Ag.) Thesis, Tamil Nadu Agricultural University, Madurai.
- Velusamy, R. and M. Manoharan, 1999. "***Characteristics of Beneficiaries of NGOs According to Gender***," Journal of Extension Education, 10(1) : 55–57.

Index

C

D

E

Index

V

W

Z